THE LORD OF THE RINGS

OFFICIAL MOVIE GUIDE

THE LORD OF THE RINGS

OFFICIAL MOVIE GUIDE

Brian Sibley

HarperCollins*Publishers*

HarperCollins*Publishers*
77–85 Fulham Palace Road,
Hammersmith, London W6 8JB
www.tolkien.co.uk

Published by HarperCollins*Publishers* 2001
1 3 5 7 9 8 6 4 2

contents

1] the road to middle-earth 6

2] the journey 14

From Book to Script 15
Seeing Tolkien's World 17
The Fellowship, Friends and Foes 30
Sean Astin, *Sam* 38
Sean Bean, *Boromir* 40
Cate Blanchett, *Galadriel* 42
Orlando Bloom, *Legolas* 44
Billy Boyd, *Pippin* 46
Sir Ian Holm, *Bilbo* 48
Christopher Lee, *Saruman* 50
Sir Ian McKellen, *Gandalf* 52
Dominic Monaghan, *Merry* 54
Viggo Mortensen, *Aragorn* 56
John Rhys-Davies, *Gimli* 58
Liv Tyler, *Arwen* 60
Hugo Weaving, *Elrond* 62
Elijah Wood, *Frodo* 64
Marton Csokas, *Celeborn* 66
Fantasy to Reality 67
A Workshop of the Fantastic 80
The One Ring 84
Of Wizard-beards and Elf-ears 96
Speaking the Languages of Middle-earth 100
Cameras in Middle-earth 102
From the Director's Chair 105
Before the Cameras Rolled 106
The Real Fellowship of the Ring 110
The Road Goes Ever On 115

1] the road to middle-earth

'I have a very, very strong affection and respect for J R R Tolkien's The Lord of the Rings, *and the films we are making really come from my vision of Tolkien's world, created in collaboration with the many other people working on this project.'*

PETER JACKSON

It would be tempting to liken Peter Jackson to a powerful wizard, conjuring up movie magic, if his build was not more suggestive of a hobbit! And perhaps that is a more appropriate analogy: since the director's sense of kinship with the small people of Middle-earth who find themselves pitted against overwhelming odds has fired his passionate and unrelenting quest to bring the literary magic of J R R Tolkien's *The Lord of the Rings* to life on the cinema screen.

'Tolkien's writing,' says Jackson, 'is so vivid that you instantly "see" the landscapes and places he is describing.' Whilst acknowledging that it will be difficult – maybe impossible – to create images that will match those of every reader, Tolkien's text remains the key source and reference in the creation of the Middle-earth depicted on film. 'Because *The Lord of the Rings* is based on such a widely read, well-loved book, we are as determined as is humanly possible not to let people down!'

'Since starting this movie,' says Jackson, 'I have read this book hundreds of times, literally word for word… Indeed, before I film a scene, I usually go back and read that chapter from the book. It is very inspiring to walk onto the set with that stuff in your head and then shoot that very scene.'

The same can be said of many other people working on the film – in front of and behind the camera. There may never have been a movie adapted from a book in which so many of the artists and technicians were as devoted to the material they were attempting to put onto film. 'From that point of view,' adds Jackson, 'the films are very much a labour of love: made *for* fans of the book, *by* fans of the book. Hopefully, it may also be a way of introducing people to Middle-earth who have never read the book. I would like to think that they might go and see the films and in seeing them experience something of the complexity, the magic and the fascinating themes found in Tolkien's book.'

Opposite: *Three wizards: Gandalf, Saruman and Jackson*

Below: *Before shooting a scene, Jackson reads the relevant passage in Tolkien's text*

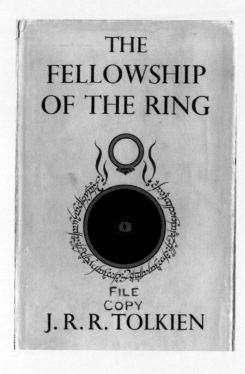

'I think *The Lord of the Rings* is one of the best stories ever written. It is a book that is eternally popular with readers of all ages.' Mr Bilbo Baggins tends to say exactly what he thinks, so it is not surprising to find Sir Ian Holm, who plays him in the film, doing likewise. Holm is not alone in being an admirer of the book. 'It is magical,' says Christopher Lee, who portrays the corrupt wizard, Saruman. 'It is a mixture of myth, legend, and what feels like almost contemporary history in that there's a sense in which the story almost parallels the behaviour and reactions, the mentalities, morals, ideals and beliefs of our world today. And the whole thing is bound together into one piece of such "magic", that there isn't any other word to describe it.'

Hugo Weaving, playing Elrond the Elf-lord of Rivendell senses in *The Lord of the Rings* genuine mythological power: 'The book draws on strands from European and world mythologies; stories that seem to have a place in our communal consciousness. That's why people reading the book – or, now, seeing the films – find an affinity with *The Lord of the Rings*: it tells, in a new form, ancient stories which still have meaning for us today.'

Indeed, John Rhys-Davies, who plays Gimli the Dwarf, sees Tolkien's mythology as meeting a common contemporary need in people: 'Many of us have an enormous hunger for adventure, for a dynamic life that can only be encountered in the world of the imagination. And Tolkien feeds that hunger with a book that is about the struggle of right and wrong, about the belief that good will triumph over evil, about courage in the face of oppression and about the willingness to sacrifice yourself for the greater good. These are the true determiners of a heroic civilization and, in our hearts, we all want to be part of just such an heroic civilization.'

'At the centre of the story,' says Elijah Wood who plays Frodo Baggins, whose quest it is, aided by his fellow hobbit Sam Gamgee, to destroy the One Ring, 'there's this little hobbit and this other little hobbit. They stand together against all odds, destroy the opposition and save Middle-earth. Although they are only a little people who would never normally be given such a responsibility, they accomplish this amazing feat, which is a reminder, perhaps, that any of us can do *anything* if we only put our mind to it.'

These are some of the qualities of Tolkien's book that have attracted many of the actors to this project. For Sir Ian Holm it was a combination of his own admiration for the book and the reaction of his thirteen-year-old son: 'As soon as he heard that I had been asked to play Bilbo, he said, "Oh my God, Dad, you are actually going to be in *The Lord of the Rings*!" Everything I've ever done in my entire career, it seems, pales into insignificance besides the fact I'm going to be in this one film!'

The Lord of the Rings *has been voted in several worldwide polls as the Book of the Twentieth Century.*

J R R Tolkien's story has its beginning in the early 1930s. John Ronald Reuel Tolkien, Professor of Anglo-Saxon at Oxford University, was busy marking examination papers when, suddenly, some words popped into his head, and onto a sheet of paper left blank by one of the examination candidates. 'In a hole in the ground', he scribbled, 'there lived a hobbit...'

An adventure began to unfold in his mind and was written down as a serial to be read to his three sons on winter evenings after tea. This was the first telling of the story we know as *The Hobbit*. The title character was a Mr Bilbo Baggins, a very well-to-do hobbit who resided at Bag End, a comfortable hobbit-hole on the Hill, in Hobbiton, in the Shire and who, like most self-respecting hobbits, would not normally have got himself involved in anything so disturbing and uncomfortable as an adventure. However, an adventure – in the form of Gandalf the wizard and thirteen dwarves – turned up on his very door step.

As a result, Bilbo found himself setting out on a dangerous quest for Dragon-gold, journeying through a land of wondrous places, peopled with strange, fabulous and terrifying beings. It was while encountering one such creature - the pale-eyed, hissing Gollum – that Bilbo chanced upon a magic ring that gave the wearer the power of invisibility.

A series of chance connections resulted in Tolkien's story becoming a book, published in 1937 by George Allen & Unwin as *The Hobbit, or There and Back Again*.

Tolkien gave the name Wilderland to the region in which Bilbo's adventures took place, but it gradually became clear that this was a part of Middle-earth, an imaginary world which Tolkien had begun to create in 1917, when he had started filling the pages of a notebook with fragments of an epic fantasy. From the entries in this book – called *The Book of Lost Tales* – grew a sprawling saga of staggering literary invention that would eventually become known as *The Silmarillion*.

In telling his sons the tale of *The Hobbit*, Tolkien drew on the mythology and history of Middle-earth, until it became clear, as he put it, that this was, indeed, 'the world into which Mr Baggins strayed'. However, Bilbo's escapades in Middle-earth turned out to be only a prologue to a more ambitious story...

So popular was *The Hobbit* that the publishers were soon asking for 'another book about the hobbit'. Within three months, Tolkien began writing a sequel. Where the first book had opened with a chapter called 'An Unexpected Party', the *new* story began with a chapter entitled 'A Long-Expected Party', in which Bilbo used his magic ring to disappear at the celebrations of his eleventy-first birthday. But the ring, it transpired, was far more powerful than readers of *The Hobbit* (or its author) might originally have guessed. For this ring was a ring of great power forged by the Dark Lord Sauron to control the races of Middle-earth.

It was to take J R R Tolkien twelve years to write the story of Bilbo's nephew Frodo and his perilous journey to the shadow-filled Land of Mordor, in order to destroy the One Ring and, with it, the power of Sauron.

Called *The Lord of the Rings*, the completed story was thought too big to be published in one volume and so appeared in three parts: *The Fellowship of the Ring* and *The Two Towers*, both published during 1954 and, in the following year, *The Return of the King*.

'Peter is making these films for the small boy that he once was who loved going to the cinema. He's giving back to film what he's received from it.'

PHILIPPA BOYENS

'It was a Friday night. I was nine years old and I was watching *King Kong* on television. That was the night when I realized what it was that I wanted to do.' Peter Jackson, director of *The Lord of the Rings Trilogy*, is recalling the first stirrings of his ambition to become a film-maker.

'Seeing the original 1933 *King Kong*,' says Jackson, 'was the first time that I felt the power of a movie to draw you out of the real world and take you to places that you would never, ever go. I was totally swallowed up by the trip to Skull Island and the tracking of King Kong and the fighting with the dinosaurs! And I knew that I wanted to make movies that had the same effect on other people as that film had on me.'

Many years later – having seen *King Kong* another forty or fifty times – there would be talk of Peter Jackson re-making that film. It was a project which never materialized; had it done so, the director might never have embarked on *The Lord of the Rings Trilogy*.

Jackson was born in Wellington, New Zealand in 1961 – appropriately, for a film-maker with a penchant for horror, on Hallowe'en. An only child with a vivid imagination, he responded to the fantastic wherever he encountered it: in books and comics, on film and television.

When he was five or six years old, the young Peter Jackson was avidly watching *Thunderbirds*, a sophisticated British television puppet series by Gerry and Sylvia Anderson. Jackson was, he remembers, 'captivated by the wonderful space-ships and amazing special effects'.

His fascination with the stop-motion model animation used in *King Kong*, led him to discover the fantasy films of Ray Harryhausen such as the memorable *Jason and the Argonauts* and, when Jackson's parents bought a Super-8 cine-camera, he immediately started making his own little fantasy home-movies.

Inspired by the prehistoric animals in *King Kong* and the mythical creatures in the films of Harryhausen, Jackson made and animated his own clay dinosaurs in a picture about a monster that destroyed a city in the style of Ray Harryhausen's *The Beast from Twenty Thousand Fathoms*. The film was entered for a local competition and, although it didn't win, fired his desire to be an animator.

However, Jackson became increasingly attracted to live-action film-making and at the age of sixteen decided to make his own vampire movie, roping in friends to play various parts in the film. In addition to being its director, he gave himself the lead role of the vampire-killer! 'It was based,' he recalls, 'on all those Hammer horror movies starring Christopher Lee and Peter Cushing that I'd been watching as a teenager! I loved the idea of making films that were based on – or inspired by – the kind of films I loved watching.'

On leaving school, Jackson went to work as an apprentice photo-lithographer, but his ambitions to get into the film business were undiminished and by the time he was twenty he had saved up enough money to buy a 16mm camera (price, second-hand, $250 NZ) and was spending his weekends making his first amateur feature film. The day-job provided funds to buy film-stock for what Jackson describes as 'this very expensive hobby', and work-mates were enlisted as cast-members, along with some of those friends who had already starred in his vampire movie.

'They all helped me,' says Jackson, 'and, over the course

of four years, we eventually made a feature film called *Bad Taste*. Although it was really only a home-movie, it enabled me to quit my job and become a full-time filmmaker.' It was a friend in the film industry who told Jackson that *Bad Taste* – which was filled with black humour and a generous helping of often amateurish special effects – might have commercial potential. A screening at the Cannes Film Festival brought praise and prizes and the film was soon heading for cult status.

Over the next few years Jackson produced a variety of projects that demonstrated a quirky taste for the bizarre combined with an impressive directorial eye: *Meet the Feebles*, a tale of ugly goings-on behind-the-scenes of a television puppet show; *Braindead*, a zombie-picture with equal measure of laughs and chills and a concluding gore-fest; *Heavenly Creatures*, a murder drama enacted in the shadowy hinterland between the real world and a fantasy realm, and *The Frighteners*, a ghost movie with a touch of attitude and a liberal dose of spooky special effects.

'If I was looking for common threads between the films I have made,' says Jackson, 'it would be that each of them was a movie that I would have liked to watch myself. Another, more obvious, thread would be the fact that all of them have made considerable use of special effects and that stems from my childhood love of that type of films. Ultimately, however, I feel very strongly that my films are about character and story.'

Jackson's stated passion for story and character and his confidence in dealing with special effects have stood him in good stead for the task of bringing Tolkien's epic tale to the screen.

'I guess,' he says, '*The Lord of the Rings Trilogy* is really the culmination of all the films I have made. It's by far the biggest project that I've tackled and something that I would not have been capable of making earlier in my career. Having made four or five movies, I now have a confidence in what I can do, including handling special effects which is important, because they could so easily be allowed to overwhelm the story. And then there's my background: that fascination with the interweaving of fantasy and reality that began when I was nine years old and sat, mesmerized, watching *King Kong…*'

'I first read and enjoyed *The Lord of the Rings* when I was about seventeen,' recalls Jackson, 'As an apprentice photo-lithographer, I had to travel from Wellington to Auckland for a six-week training course. It was a twelve-hour train journey, so I took a copy *The Lord of the Rings* with me to pass the time.'

The book made an immediate impact on the young Jackson: 'My first thought was: "I can't wait until somebody makes a movie of this book, because *I'd* like to see it!" So, I waited twenty odd years and, as nobody else made that film I'd been wanting to see, I ended up making it myself!'

It was 1995, Peter Jackson and Fran Walsh were

completing work on *The Frighteners* and considering future projects. 'The idea of doing *The Lord of the Rings* came up,' says Jackson, 'I still had those strong memories of reading the book twenty years earlier and still thought it would make a great movie. I just couldn't understand why nobody else seemed to be doing anything about it.'

Continued speculation resulted in Jackson deciding to find out – once and for all – who owned the film rights to the book and whether anyone was trying to do anything with them. The answer was that the rights in the epic were held by Saul Zaentz, who had obtained them from Tolkien towards the end of the author's life and who had produced the 1978 animated film that had been based on the stories.

At the time, Zaentz was making a Miramax film of *The English Patient* and, as Jackson had a relationship with the same production company, a telephone conversation with Harvey Weinstein of Miramax led to another between Weinstein and Zaentz. 'From that seed,' says Jackson, 'things happened and somehow we ended up with the opportunity to make the film.'

It was to take some time, however, for that opportunity to become a workable venture. Whilst Miramax had originally discussed the project in terms of *two* movies, they subsequently decided that the story would need to be told as a single two-hour film.

Jackson, who was decidedly unhappy with this proposal, had the option of finding an alternative studio partner. It was New Line Cinema who courageously stepped into the breach and agreed to back the project as two films. At last, Jackson could think in terms of bringing Tolkien's book to the screen as a trilogy of movies.

The challenge facing Jackson was enormous: that of bringing to life one of the best-loved books in world literature (a book, moreover, that is over one thousand pages long) with a sufficient sense of realism to convince movie-goers of the existence of an entire other world.

It is this quest that has been the motivation at every stage in the planning and filming of *The Lord of the Rings*. Whilst many people may think of Middle-earth as a fantasy world, that is not the view of Supervising Art Director Dan Hennah: 'It's not a fantasy world, it's a *real* world, full of real

Peter Jackson and Dan Hennah check out a digital image on a 'clamshell'

people and real animals, creatures and races that are quite different from one another. You have to think of it as being more than just a figment of Tolkien's imagination, he has created a world that millions of people have read about and believe in. And it is that world that we're trying to reproduce as faithfully as possible.'

Much of this task fell to Weta Workshop Ltd and Weta Digital Ltd, the New Zealand physical and digital effects studios named after a large indigenous insect – the weta – which has been around for some one hundred million years. Richard Taylor is its director: 'In taking on a project like this you have to appreciate that you are dabbling in people's dreams and visions, in what many strongly feel to be their culture. Yet whilst the written word is as big as the human imagination, as expansive as whatever we conceive when we read the text, the film image can only be as big as whatever you can encapsulate in a second of footage on screen.'

This is one of several reasons why it has taken almost fifty years for *The Lord of the Rings* to be made into a live-action movie. Another is that potential film-makers in the past would have been seriously inhibited by the constraints of attempting to encompass the entire book within the time-span of a single motion picture. Certainly that was Peter Jackson's view: 'Who would want to adapt the most beloved

Jackson directs Lee as the wizard, Saruman

book of all time in a way that obliges you to cut out half of the good stuff and squash the rest into just one film? Making three movies has allowed us to be so much more faithful in how we have adapted the book.'

Modern technology has also enabled Peter Jackson and his colleagues to bring *The Lord of the Rings* to the screen with a visual realism previously unthinkable. 'The advent of modern computer visual effects,' says Jackson, 'means that we are now able to show the sort of images which the story calls for with a flourish and a flair that, hitherto, would have been impossible.'

With the aid of cutting-edge computer technologies and an astonishing attention to detailing in sets, costumes and make-up, the film-makers have produced a visionary repre-

sentation of Tolkien's Middle-earth. 'We had to create an expansive world,' says Dan Hennah, 'something that would spread beyond the four corners of the movie screen.'

'If we make a film that has the heart and the spirit of the book,' says Jackson, 'so that the characters come alive and feel real, the way they do when you read the story; if we can create the diversity and visual excitement you get from the books and make it totally accessible to an audience whether or not they've ever *read* those books, then we will have made a good movie.'

Actor Christopher Lee has no doubts about the success of the films which he sees as having the popular appeal of George Lucas' *Star Wars* movies combined with the creative magnitude of D W Griffith's *Birth of a Nation*: 'I honestly believe that the impact of this production will be greater than almost anything ever seen in the cinema.'

2] THE JOURNEY

from book to script

'**N**ow I won't have *The Lord of the Rings* to go and read on a wet Sunday – I'll no longer be able to pick up the book and re-enter that world.' Philippa Boyens can be forgiven for feeling a little melancholy, for her work – with Fran Walsh and Peter Jackson – on adapting J R R Tolkien's book for the screen has been a mammoth undertaking. 'We simply haven't stopped reading it. There isn't a day that's gone by in three years when we haven't picked it up and read how Tolkien wrote a scene or described a particular character.'

For Fran Walsh, whose first recollections of *The Lord of the Rings* date from having the book read to her in childhood ('It always seems to have been part of my imaginative life'), the process of translating a much-loved book into a series of filmable screenplays has been a fascinating challenge: 'There is so much material in the book, so many threads to the narrative: there's a fantastic tale of loyalty, love and friendship at the heart of Frodo and Sam's saga; there's the equally compelling romantic story of Aragorn and Arwen and, beyond that, the vast arena of war and the struggle between the various races of Middle-earth and the evil of Sauron. That is a huge tapestry.'

Their approach to adapting the book, says Fran Walsh, has been a mutual understanding that what they were dealing with was not a work of 'fantasy' but a piece of 'pre-history': 'The true joy for me is that it feels *real*. That was the starting place for thinking how we might adapt it, to preserve that and to give life and breath to the characters and weight to the material. Along the way, of course, we have had to make choices about what could be kept for screen story-telling and what had to be discarded.'

That has been easier said than done. 'The decision about what to cut and what to leave in,' says Peter Jackson, 'is obviously a very difficult one, but the language of cinema is different to the language of the written word: it has different needs and sometimes requires a different pace, a different structure. So we worked on adapting a scenario out of Tolkien's novel that we felt would work best on film.'

The process began with Peter Jackson and Fran Walsh who had previously collaborated on the scripts for *The Frighteners*, *Meet the Feebles*, *Braindead* and *Heavenly Creatures*, the latter of which had secured them an Academy Award nomination for Best Screenplay. Together, they made a detailed breakdown of the plot as a single, complete story and invited Philippa Boyens to read it and give her comments. Boyens agreed, but with some nervousness: 'As a Tolkien fan, I just couldn't see how anybody could make this book into a movie, but I was immediately astonished by how much they had managed to capture in that initial treatment. And amazingly, looking back on it in terms of the shaping of the major events, that breakdown still stands today as being, essentially, what Peter has put onto film.'

Opposite: *Frodo and Sam leave the Shire*

Below: *The streets of Bree*

Bilbo gives his farewell speech

Detailed story sessions between the trio would be followed by intensive script-writing. 'For over a year,' says Boyens, 'it was Fran and I shut away, working together in a room.' Before any scene was written – and many times while it was *being* written – Jackson was intensely involved in deciding how a sequence should be approached or how a particular character might be used and developed.

Throughout the filming of all three pictures, the scripting process remained, in Peter Jackson's words, 'organic', with countless re-writes and endless refinements right up to the moment of committing a scene to film: 'Peter continued overseeing and helping shape the moment-by-moment storytelling,' recalls Boyens, 'especially the big cinematic sequences, what might be called "the big print" in the script.'

'What I found so amazing about those scripts,' says Associate Producer, Rick Porras, 'is that immediately – even in early drafts – they embodied the tenor of the books, captured the substance of Tolkien's writing, had all those moments that I found to be important and, above all, that affected me in the same way that the books had affected me. That is a really

wonderful gift that we've been given by the writers.' Richard Taylor whose company Weta Workshop Ltd has had the task of visualizing on screen many of the images embodied in the screenplays, has nothing but praise for the scripts: 'There's no doubt in my mind that they've written the best scripts that could have been extrapolated from Tolkien's written word.'

As the process of turning Tolkien's book into screenplays developed, the film-makers increasingly drew on the original text. 'When we first started writing these scripts,' says Peter Jackson, 'we assumed that we would have to simplify and modernize the language, because that was what a modern film would require. On the contrary, however, with each subsequent draft of the screenplays, we have gone further and further into Tolkien's language, because it is beautiful and evocative and, when spoken by good actors, comes alive in a way that is really fresh and exciting.'

Nevertheless, cuts had to be made and scenes amalgamated or moved to create necessary dramatic tensions. Dialogue was sometimes 'borrowed' from one part of the book to provide lines for a character in a scene somewhere else, and occasionally new dialogue had to be written, 'in the style of Tolkien'. One or two characters in the original book have not, finally, found their way onto the screen, while others, notably the few female characters, have been given stronger roles in the film than they have in the original text.

Throughout the entire process of bringing this world-famous book to the cinema, Peter Jackson has kept one, over-riding, principle in mind: 'My primary job has been to make three good movies, as opposed to making three movies that are totally faithful to the books. Nevertheless, I fully accept that I have a responsibility not to disappoint those many people who love the books. Which is why we have really tried not to lose anything that we feel is key or important to the books and why, almost without exception, all those things that are memorable and vivid from reading the books are there in the movies.'

seeing tolkien's world

'Tolkien wrote at great length describing these worlds, these cities, these environments,' says Weta Workshop's Richard Taylor, 'but also, very fortuitously for us, he enhanced the written word with his own illustrations.'

When he submitted the manuscript of *The Hobbit* to his publishers, Tolkien also sent several hand-drawn maps and later a number of pictures he had made for the story whilst telling it to his family. The illustrations were highly stylized and rather exotic and included views of Hobbiton, Bag End and Rivendell. These were the first visualizations of Middle-earth.

No illustrations were included in *The Lord of the Rings* when, volume by volume, it was published in 1954 and 1955: however, as the tale developed, Tolkien made sketches and finished drawings of some of locations in the story, such as the Brandywine Ferry used by the hobbits in the film to escape the Black Riders, Saruman's stronghold at Isengard, the gates to the Mines of Moria and the Golden Wood of Lothlórien.

With the book's growing popularity in the 1960s and 70s, a number of artists in Britain and America were inspired to use Middle-earth imagery on posters and record-album sleeves while fantasy calendars began featuring interpretations of well-known characters and episodes from *The Lord of the Rings*.

Although numerous Tolkien pictures found their way into print, it was not until 1991 that a fully illustrated edition of *The Lord of the Rings* was published with fifty watercolour paintings by the English artist, Alan Lee who, with fellow Tolkien illustrator, John Howe, has played a major role in creating the visual realization of Middle-earth in Peter Jackson's film trilogy.

The Lord of the Rings has also inspired any number of artefacts from character candles and decorative plates to porcelain figurines and board-games and has repeatedly been celebrated by the performing arts. The songs and poems have been set to music by various composers, the author himself recorded extracts from his writings and several of his books have since been read – in full or in edited form – by a number of distinguished actors.

Radio versions of *The Lord of the Rings* have been broadcast in America and in Britain beginning with a dramatized reading of *The Fellowship of the Ring*, broadcast shortly after the book's publication. In 1981, the BBC broadcast a twenty-six week serialization that received great acclaim and starred Ian Holm as Frodo, a piece of casting that, twenty years later, led Peter Jackson to offer Sir Ian the role of Frodo's Uncle Bilbo, in the film of *The Lord of the Rings*.

A cartoon television film of *The Hobbit* was made in 1977 and the following year saw the release of the first of two planned animated films based on *The Lord of the Rings*, directed by animator Ralph (*Fritz the Cat*) Bakshi. The film was only

Alan Lee by John Howe

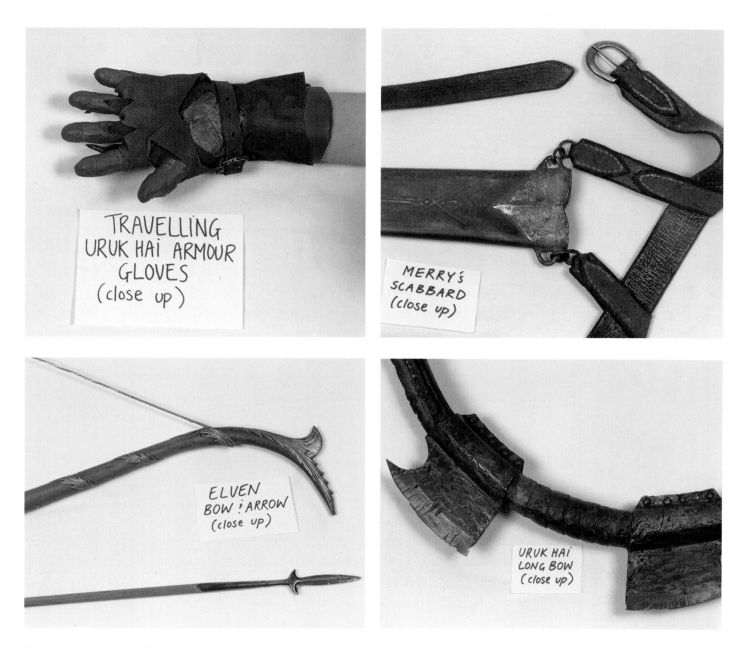

Clockwise from top left: Travelling Uruk-hai armour gloves (close up); Merry's scabbard (close up); Uruk-hai long bow (close up); Elven bow and arrow (close up).

> *'The word I would use to describe the fine work that's gone into every aspect of this production is obsessive. Actually, it's more than an obsession, it is born of love.'*

moderately successful and the concluding part of the story was later made by other hands as *The Return of the King*.

Despite its growth in stature – from being the bible of the hippie-culture, via a huge fan-following to being a work that was recently voted 'The Book of the Century' – *The Lord of the Rings* has nevertheless eluded successful translation into the most popular medium of our age – film.

Now, at long last, comes a series of live-action movies bringing the world of Middle-earth to life with a dramatic and compelling realism that seeks to do justice to the extraordinary imaginative powers of J R R Tolkien.

'The word I would use to describe the fine work that's gone into every aspect of this production is obsessive. Actually, it's more than an obsession, it is born of love.'

This is the view of the man behind the camera. Not Peter Jackson or any of the camera crew on *The Lord of the Rings*, but Costa Botes, the video documentarian who has been filming the film-makers at work since the earliest days of the project.

Having witnessed the process of bringing Tolkien's world to life on the screen, Botes' view of the film is that of both a film-maker and an outside observer: 'These people are pouring all their time and efforts into creating the whole texture of this world and are coming up with things that will make the audience's mouths drop open.'

The driving principle has been the desire to achieve authenticity: 'It has been remarked,' says Peter Jackson, 'that if you want to know more about any aspect of the story of *The Lord of the Rings*, you simply scrape away the surface and you'll always find more information, going back thousands of years. Tolkien created all that historical material and whilst it is difficult for us to put that into a movie, it is vital that the film is seen as being more than just characters in costumes walking around in a New Zealand landscape.'

The film-makers researched Tolkien's many writings about Middle-earth and employed Tolkien illustrators, Alan Lee and John Howe, to serve as conceptual artists on the project. Designs conceived for the film have then been realized by Richard Taylor and his colleagues at Weta Workshop. 'These are the people,' says Peter Jackson, 'who have really led the charge in creating the different cultures of the various races of Middle-earth.'

'Culture is based in detail,' says Richard Taylor; 'in generations of characters, of people, of species, building on top of the past generation's work.' By building up what Taylor refers to as 'layer upon layer' of detail in the design of everything from the sets and props to costumes and make-up, the films' designers have suggested something of the history, cultural background to the people and places of Middle-earth. 'The Elves, the Dwarves and hobbits of Middle-earth,' says Peter Jackson, 'all live in their own isolated communities. And, just as in our world everybody's culture – European, American, South American, African, Australian – represents the evolution of those people through history, so it is in Middle-earth. Which is why we have taken so much care in building cultural histories for the characters in these films.'

Whilst admitting that much of their work will go unno-ticed or, at best, only register 'subconsciously' with movie audiences, Richard Taylor believes that if those design elements were missing, the overall look of the film would be the poorer and that the atmosphere of filmed history, so much a part of Peter Jackson's vision for the pictures, could not have been fully conveyed.

The practical outworking of this approach has meant a vast amount of largely unsung creativity: 'There is not a buckle,' says Taylor, 'that isn't branded with the coat of arms of a particular army. Every rivet-head is detailed in some way. Every belt is hand-tooled to feel like it has been touched by the craftsmanship of the species that wears it. And, hopefully, by doing this, the audience will gain a richer, more fulfilled, perspective of the cultures that have gone on for thousands of years to generate the look of the period represented in the film.'

'Maybe the camera won't pick up on it all,' says Production Designer Grant Major, 'but it is all there, nevertheless, in the interest of creating these real environments inhabited by real people.'

Elven art: a detail from the Rivendell set

'Even though we are right down here at the bottom of the world,' says New Zealand-born Peter Jackson, 'we have mountains, forests and fields, rivers, lakes and waterfalls that have a familiar yet slightly fantastical appearance.'

This quality of 'unfamiliar familiarity' is something that Sir Ian McKellen responded to on arriving in New Zealand to play Gandalf: 'Everything here is more magnificent. The landscape is familiar in the sense it's been formed by rain – just as Tolkien's Oxfordshire was – but the vegetation is unusual and the mountains seem so much sharper. If you're looking for what the poets used to call "the awful"' – a sense of awe – then that is what you find in New Zealand. And it's wild in a way that England isn't wild.'

Other members of the cast agree. 'New Zealand is the ideal place to shoot these films,' notes Cate Blanchett, 'the land mass is so young, so savage, so untamed and unruly, all of which makes it special.' Elijah Wood adds: 'New Zealand is gorgeous! I don't really think that there's anywhere else we could have filmed this movie unless we had travelled to lots of different places around the world. Every element of Middle-earth is contained in New Zealand. It is perfect. There are so many different geographical landscapes: mountains, woods, marshes, desert areas, rolling hills – and the sea. Everything, in fact, described in *The Lord of the Rings*.'

For John Rhys-Davies the New Zealand landscape is particularly suited to a film that does not conform to the look of a conventional Hollywood movie: 'The "Hollywood touch" would be quite wrong for this picture. Tolkien was writing about a different world, a different land, a primitive land and a primitive time in history. New Zealand – breathtakingly beautiful – is just perfect for that.'

For Scottish-born actor Billy Boyd, who plays Pippin, the panoramas of New Zealand recalled his homeland: 'There are parts that are really like Scotland – only bigger! Maybe it's Scotland as seen by a hobbit!' Boyd also sees a parallel between the way in which the many terrains unfolding on the eye through the three films and the ever-changing landscape of Tolkien's story: 'Think of the size of Middle-earth compared to the Shire, where the hobbits live, which is a country in its own right: the landscape just keeps opening up and opening up and every place is new and different. So the folk in the Shire have no idea that Elves live in trees in Lothlórien, or that Dwarves once lived in a huge underground city beneath the mountains.'

This sense of wonder and discovery, of vast distances and long journeys is central to the book and to the films. For Peter Jackson, the landscapes depicted in the film trilogy needed to fit with Tolkien's vision of Middle-earth: '*The Lord of the Rings* is not a fantasy *per se*,' he explains, 'Tolkien wrote the book as a mythic pre-history of a Europe existing in a

dark age, long since forgotten. So I wanted to set the film in a slightly surreal version of a European landscape – which is exactly what New Zealand offers.'

For more than a year before filming began, Location Production Manager Richard Sharkey, and Location Supervisor Robin Murphy, accompanied Peter Jackson as he travelled the length and breadth of both North and South Islands, scouting possible locations. Working closely with New Zealand's Department of Conservation, the film crew filmed at more than seventy locations (not counting studios) during the making of the trilogy: from rural farmland to sweeping rivers and snow-capped mountain peaks.

Video Documentarian Costa Botes followed Peter Jackson and his team: 'The locations were simply too good to ignore and whilst, in general, they've been chosen for their scenic splendour, other – rather more surprising – locations have been used. Peter has shot scenes in places no one would have thought of using, many of them around the city of Wellington, such as trees in a park or behind a playground where, if you looked a little to the left or right you would realize you were in the middle of a city, but from a particu-

Left: *The Stone Trolls, from Alan Lee's illustrated edition of* The Lord of the Rings

lar camera-angle you are in Middle-earth!'

In addition to providing a variety of vastly different landscapes, many of them within reasonably easy access of one another, New Zealand offered an unspoiled environment with landscapes relatively uncluttered with the impedimenta of human civilization: no power pylons straddling the hills, no motorways ripping great tears of tarmac across farmland.

As Conceptual Artist John Howe observes, New Zealand has fewer indications of ancient human presence that are so familiar within the European landscape: 'Here there were no castles, no ruins, nothing to be taken into account; just this ancient ecosystem with its slightly odd-shaped rocks and trees. Whatever places were needed – age-old buildings, the remnants of lost civilizations – they had to be created from scratch and that gave us a wonderful freedom. Peter told us: "If you can draw it, we can make it." And that is what we have done. And the fabulous New Zealand landscape and the villages, towns and cities we have built in them have an organic wholeness.'

'Look around and you can see Alan Lee and John Howe's influences in everything we do. They have touched every part of what we make.'

TANIA RODGER, MANAGER OF WETA WORKSHOP LTD

'These paintings capture the melancholy feeling and bittersweet mood of *The Lord of the Rings*,' Peter Jackson is leafing through a three-volume set of Tolkien's book illustrated with watercolours by the English artist, Alan Lee. 'Flying in the face of a lot of fantasy art that has really been appropriated by the heavy metal culture, Alan Lee depicts Middle-earth as a very real world.'

It was in 1995, when Jackson seriously began considering how to approach the filming of *The Lord of the Rings*, that he came across Alan Lee's illustrated edition of the book: 'We didn't originally buy the books for the pictures, but all the time we were thinking about how we would adapt the story for the screen, we were thumbing through these volumes

Rivendell, from Alan Lee's illustrated edition of The Lord of the Rings

and these paintings began making a huge impression on us and the more familiar we became with Tolkien's world, the more we came to feel that we couldn't imagine the places in the story as looking anything other than how Alan shows them.'

When the film began to become a reality, Jackson and his colleagues decided that they should try to locate Alan Lee

Alan Lee adds a finishing touch to Rivendell

and see if the artist was interested in working on the project. Although Lee had begun his film career as a conceptual designer on Ridley Scott's film, *Legend*, and had worked on the movie *Erik the Viking* most of his time since studying graphic design at the Ealing School of Art in London, had been devoted to book illustration. With his particular fascination for Norse legends and Celtic myths, his books on *Castles* and *Faeries* and his illustrations for the story of Odysseus and the Welsh epic, *The Mabinogion*, Alan Lee has established himself as an artist with a unerring eye for depicting the fantastic as if it were a part of our everyday lives.

Peter Jackson eventually tracked Lee down to a small

A Lee original finds its way into the set

village near Dartmoor in the west country of England. 'He's a very sweet, rather shy chap,' says Jackson, 'and we really weren't sure if he would want to be involved, so we were absolutely thrilled and delighted when he said that he'd be interested in helping us.'

'It came out of the blue,' says Alan Lee, recalling the day on which he received a video copy of Peter Jackson's *Heavenly Creatures* and a letter from the film-maker telling him about the project: 'I was impressed by the fact that he wanted to be true to the spirit of the books and to try and create a believable world with real landscapes and places. The invitation to go to New Zealand arrived at one of the rare times when I didn't have any contracts looming and could be free within a few weeks. So, I phoned Peter and said I'd go out there.' It was suggested that Lee might be needed for between twelve and twenty weeks, but almost three years later he was still there and, he says, 'beginning to feel like something of a Kiwi!'

Producer, Barrie Osborne describes Alan Lee's unique contribution to *The Lord of the Rings* as 'invaluable and inspirational' and – coming as it does from a European, rather than a South Pacific, tradition – giving a particular design quality to the movies. 'As the film developed,' says Production Designer Grant Major, 'Alan's rich, illustrative style really became our Bible and has influenced everything we've done. He has enabled us, even though we're halfway round the world, to tap into a depth of European culture.'

Alan Lee's approach to the design of the film was rooted in Tolkien's text: 'When I'm illustrating any book, I read and re-read and just let the images appear. Then, when I'm drawing, I try to get as close as I can to those images that I got when I was reading and simply trust that they will be close enough to the images that everybody else has experienced.'

Working closely with Peter Jackson, Alan Lee and fellow artist, John Howe, set to work visualizing a Middle-earth that had that essential sense of realism and authenticity: 'We tried to give depth to the design, so that you felt there was a history to it, that it wasn't just something that had been put together for the purposes of making a film but that these places had been developing over thousands of years.'

The process of turning those designs into sets and costumes was a fascinating experience for someone who was primarily an illustrator and Alan Lee enjoyed the thrill of seeing his two-dimensional designs become three-dimensional reality: 'It's been hugely exciting. I've always tried to make my pictures believable, but to see your pictures take on life has been extraordinary!'

And as Lee's images of Middle-earth graduated from drawing-board visions to physical places, the artist would be there, sometimes minutes before the actors arrived, adding one or two finishing touches, working in a little extra detail before filming commenced. 'I can't resist getting involved,' says Lee, 'I'm there and I just have to pick up the paintbrush and join in!'

'John Howe's art work tends to be like a freeze-frame from a film. He is very good at capturing action at an exciting moment, holding it and painting it.'

Peter Jackson is looking at a painting of the Black Riders, emissaries of the Dark Lord, being swept away by the flood-waters at the Ford of Bruinen when they are in pursuit of Frodo on his way to Rivendell. 'So much of John's artwork feels like a moment in the movie.'

Jackson particularly responded to Howe's 'vision of evil' and several sequences in *The Fellowship of the Ring* such as the cataclysmic confrontation between Gandalf and the monstrous Balrog in the Mines of Moria are, in many ways, three-dimensional visualizations of some of the artist's most dramatic paintings.

'It's been extremely exciting,' says John Howe, speaking from his home in Switzerland. 'Doing a set of drawings and then seeing them sculpted as life-size figures is a very heady experience for someone who has always worked alone and only on a flat surface! I love treating movement and volumes and here it all was, taking shape, right before my eyes, through the talents of sculptors and computer artists at Weta Workshop.'

Born in Vancouver, British Columbia, John Howe is established as one of the most successful interpreters of Tolkien's world. His powerful depictions of some of the most

dramatic episodes in *The Lord of the Rings* have been reproduced on posters and calendars and used as book-jacket designs.

The invitation for Howe to work on the film took the form of a telephone call that, due to the time-difference between New Zealand and Switzerland, came at a very early hour one morning. 'It was three or four o'clock and, needless to say, I didn't get much sleep the rest of that night! My initial reaction was mixed: I was caught between wanting to be involved in such an ambitious project and wondering if it really could be done and whether I could ever come to terms with working inside a huge team. By morning I had made up my mind to say "Yes"! The alternative - to say "It can't possibly be done properly, so don't get involved" - was simply unthinkable.'

Howe's contribution to *The Lord of the Rings* is multi-

faceted: from specific images that have transferred directly from his artwork to the screen – such as that of Gandalf arriving at Frodo's home in Hobbiton – to hundreds of new inspirational sketches that have helped create the many extraordinary settings in the story and some of the darkest and most terrifying moments in the films.

The artist's specialist knowledge of the medieval world was particularly appreciated by Weta Workshop's Richard Taylor: 'Having John arrive was like the arrival of an expert who had stepped right out of the Middle Ages and into our time! John's passion for this period infected us all and undoubtedly drove us to greater heights in our work.'

During the period in which he worked in New Zealand, John Howe got through dozens of pencils: 'I kept all the stubs as they got worn down and, by the end, there were enough to fill a jam-jar!'

Above: *John Howe*
Opposite: *The Dark Tower by John Howe*

It took a little time to adjust to the process of working with film-makers and meeting their needs: 'I generally have a rather messy sketching style, but in this case it was important, especially for landscapes and architecture, to slow down and take the time to render details. But any given drawing would start somewhere on a big sheet of paper, and might then grow in whatever direction it led. Some pictures ended up yards long!'

For an artist with a taste for turning the creatures of fantasy into living, breathing beings, the opportunities presented by working on the film were endless: 'Watching the first fell beasts – the winged creatures used as steeds by Sauron's servants – taking shape in the computers, was amazing! I was thinking, "This is great! I'll never again have to draw things like this from scratch!" No more long hours trying to get it right on paper, I'll just phone Weta Digital and say: "One fell beast, please, three-quarters back-view, from above, wings up!"'

the fellowship, friends and foes

'I thought, well, okay, I've put my best foot forward, I've done the best that I can possibly do to convey my passion for this role and to portray it in a new way.'

ELIJAH WOOD, ON HOW HE SET ABOUT LANDING THE ROLE OF FRODO.

Casting three movies, the first of which features no less than fifteen major roles, was a crucial, early challenge for Peter Jackson, Fran Walsh and their four Casting Directors, Victoria Burrows, John Hubbard, Liz Mullane and Ann Robinson.

Although Elijah Wood had been asked to audition for the film, the young American actor was reluctant to do so. 'They wanted me to go into a casting director's office in Los Angeles, to be videoed doing my audition against a white background. But auditions are difficult and office atmospheres are so sterile that I really didn't feel comfortable about doing that.' Wood's solution was to make his own video – on location! Not having access to the script (on which a tight hold was being kept), Elijah had to read and learn the script at the casting director's offices. Then, hiring a costume from an LA costumiers, the young actor enlisted the help of a couple of friends, one of whom had a video camera and the trio headed off into the Los Angeles hills where they found a location to shoot a couple of Frodo's scenes. They filmed a number of takes from different angles and, that night, edited the sequence together. The following day, Elijah dropped off the tape so that it could be sent on to the director. 'I felt that it wasn't just an audition tape; it was something that said: "This is *me* as a *hobbit*—" I just hoped that it would convey my passion for the role and for the films.'

It worked and Elijah Wood was cast as Frodo. 'What can I say about Elijah?' muses Peter Jackson. 'Elijah is playing Frodo as if he actually were a hobbit caught in these circumstances and dealing with them in the only way that he possibly can – *as* a hobbit. You feel, seeing the film, that it's not acting or performance, which makes it very real. I can't possibly imagine anybody else in the world who would be better suited for the role of Frodo Baggins.'

Another member of the cast who set out with some determination to secure a role in the film was veteran actor, Christopher Lee, who plays the cunning and deceitful wizard, Saruman: 'I did something that I've never done in fifty-three years in the profession. I was working on a film in Lithuania in which I was playing a wizard and when I heard that Peter Jackson – whom I had met – was going to direct *The Lord of the Rings*, I sent him a photograph of myself, bearded and dressed as a wizard hoping that it might jog his memory.'

'Finding an actor to play Saruman could have been difficult,' admits Peter

Jackson, 'he has to have enormous strength and wisdom but he also has to have an arrogance and a contempt and to convey that you need an actor who is not "acting powerful", but who has that inherent authority in their stature, in their voice. Christopher Lee is an actor who, over the years, has shown those qualities as well as having that wonderful, silky, sinister voice that is perfect for the character of Saruman.'

When Peter Jackson and Fran Walsh next visited London they met with Christopher Lee and asked if he would read an extract from the script for them: 'This was something else I hadn't done for years and years and years! Would I mind reading something – I couldn't memorize it on the spot, so I *had* to read it - and would I mind being videoed at the same time? So, of course, I said "No, not at all..." If it had been any other film, I wouldn't have done it, but some opportunities you don't turn down!'

The casting of Sir Ian McKellen as Gandalf, the other dynamic wizard of Middle-earth, also came about as a result of a meeting with Jackson and Walsh. 'Peter stressed that he was planning an illustrative, as opposed to a stylized, production,' reflects Sir Ian, 'and that the acting had to fit in with that. Since it wasn't going to be the stuff of fairy-tale, the wizards had to be believable people.'

McKellen discovered that Peter Jackson and Fran Walsh had a very clear image of Gandalf in mind: 'Their Gandalf was the Gandalf in the illustrations by John Howe: the robes, the tall hat, the long beard. Whilst they seemed convinced that I could act the part in the way they saw it, they did add that they were hoping to be convinced by their make-up department that I could also look like their Gandalf!' Fortunately the make-up department successfully completed the transformation.

Jackson is full of praise for the English knight's performance: 'Sir Ian McKellen brilliantly combines the two elements of Gandalf's character: power and humility. His standing as a wonderful Shakespearean actor gives him the stature which Gandalf needs, but he also has a softness and the most extraordinary twinkle in his eye! Sir Ian is able to make that instantaneous leap between the different facets of Gandalf's personality, switching – within seconds – from being the gentle, grandfather-like, figure to suddenly being

Opposite: *Christopher Lee as Saruman*
Below: *Sir Ian McKellen as Gandalf*

the frighteningly powerful wizard.'

Sean Astin, who plays Sam Gamgee, was driving his car through Los Angeles when his cell-phone rang. It was his agent telling him that Peter Jackson was going to be auditioning for a trilogy of films based on *The Lord of the Rings*. 'I spun my car around,' remembers Astin, 'and without even letting her finish the sentence, I went straight to a Barnes & Noble bookshop, got a copy and started reading!'

Although he hadn't previously read *The Lord of the Rings*, Astin knew *The Hobbit* and knew that if New Line Cinema were behind the project it was going to be big. He also knew and admired the films of Peter Jackson and was keen to work for the director. Whilst an audition was being arranged, Astin steeped himself in Tolkien's saga and found himself captivated by the imaginative sweep of the story: 'Little did I know, as I powered through *The Lord of the Rings*, that there would be this whole world for me to become immersed in: both

imaginatively, in reading the book, and then, physically, while trying to bring that book to life in the films.'

Character by character, the cast was assembled: Ian Holm, another English theatrical knight who, two decades earlier, had played Frodo in a highly-praised BBC radio serialization, was invited to play Frodo's Uncle Bilbo, the hobbit whose exploits, years before, had led to the finding of the One Ring.

Two of Hollywood's most popular actresses, Cate Blanchett and Liv Tyler, were cast as the Lady Galadriel and the Elf-maiden, Arwen. 'Cate,' says Peter Jackson, 'has played Galadriel as quite a scary character in that she herself is terrified of the temptation offered by the Ring and Liv has brought a wonderful ethereal quality to the role of Arwen, really showing the pain of an immortal who is prepared to

Above: *Gimli, Pippin, Boromir and Legolas*
Opposite: *The mysterious 'Strider'*

give up her immortality for the man that she loves.'

British actors John Rhys-Davies and Sean Bean were enlisted to play two members of the Fellowship of the Ring: Gimli and Boromir. Australian actor Hugo Weaving joined the by now starry cast as Elrond and relative newcomers Orlando Bloom, Dominic Monaghan and Billy Boyd were cast as Legolas and as Frodo's hobbit travelling companions, Merry and Pippin.

For Viggo Mortensen, the invitation to play the crucial, central human character of Aragorn came only after filming had begun. Stuart Townsend, the Irish actor who starred in the 1997 film *Shooting Fish*, had been cast in the role, but 'creative differences' between actor and director had resulted in a last-minute decision to re-cast. 'Basically,' recalls Viggo, 'I got a call: "Do you want go to New Zealand for fourteen months to film *The Lord of the Rings*?" Just, you know, this famous epic trilogy! And my first reaction was "No!" Obviously I'd heard of Tolkien and *The Lord of the Rings*, but

I hadn't read the book, and I certainly hadn't read the script; I usually like to have a lot more time to prepare for a major role; and I really didn't want to be away from my family for that long. I have to say, it didn't sound like a very wise move to me at all!'

Fortunately for Peter Jackson − and for movie-going audiences − other people managed to change Viggo's mind: 'My son said I was crazy and that I'd got to do it, even if I was going to be gone a long time. So, there I am on the plane for New Zealand reading that enormous, telephone directory-sized book and then the scripts and, a couple of days later, I'm filming. I continued to feel unprepared but at least I didn't have much time to get nervous, which was probably good!'

'I didn't envy the guy when he arrived,' says Video Documentarian Costa Botes: 'Viggo walked into a very tense situation, threw himself into his role amazingly and quickly won the respect of everyone on the crew.' Botes well remembers Viggo Mortensen's first day on set; the crew were busy shooting the hobbits' arrival at the Prancing Pony at Bree, the inn where they encounter a mysterious character called Strider who later reveals himself to be Aragorn: 'The filming was going on at the far end of the set when I noticed this figure in a dark hood, smoking a pipe, sitting in another corner of the set altogether. Then I realized: it was Viggo. He wasn't required in the scene, he was just sitting there, observing the vibe, he was actually "being" Strider, being the outsider, the lonely man in the corner that no one spoke to.'

With a number of important supporting roles and the first of several armies of extras, the casting for *The Fellowship of the Ring* was complete. 'Looking on,' says Costa Botes, 'day by day, from the start, as each cast member arrived and began work, my general feeling was how incredibly well those characters were cast. Without exception, the actors slipped into their roles like a hand into a glove and, physically, many of them look as if they had just stepped out of one of Alan Lee's book illustrations! It's quite uncanny!'

Eventually a number of other distinguished players − among them, Miranda Otto, Bernard Hill, Andy Serkis, John Noble, Karl Urban, David Wenham and Brad Dourif − would join the project for the second and third movies, making *The Lord of the Rings Trilogy* one of the most impressively cast film ventures in many years.

sean astin
sam

'**H**e is a gardener: that's the first thing to remember about him.' Sean Astin is talking about Sam Gamgee, his character in *The Lord of the Rings Trilogy*. 'As I read the book, I was looking for keys to unlock Sam's personality. He is a gardener and he's loyal and honest, and sometimes he gets scared. These are very basic things about Sam that I have tried to I embody in playing him.'

Astin's parents are the actor and director, John Astin, and actress, Patty Duke with whom he made his television debut in 1981. Inevitably, as a young actor, he has also 'played' a number of sons including Michael Douglas and Kathleen Turner's boy in Danny DeVito's *The War of the Roses* and Izzy, Sam Shepard and Susan Sarandon's son in *Safe Passage*.

In a succession of movies since Astin's first film role as Mikey in Richard Donner's teen adventure, *The Goonies*, Astin has demonstrated considerable dramatic talent in a filmography that ranges from zany comedies (Dudley Moore's *Like Father, Like Son*) to hard-edged dramas such as *Where the Day Takes You*. His more than thirty feature film appearances include, *Staying Together*, *Encino Man*, *Memphis Belle*, *Courage Under Fire*, *Bulworth* and the title-role in *Rudy*. He received the Best Actor award for *Low Life* at the Fort Lauderdale Film Festival.

In addition to acting, Astin has embarked on a parallel career as a director with two short films: *On My Honor* about an American and a Vietnamese soldier, and *Kangaroo Court*, an inner-city drama starring Gregory Hines and Michael O'Keefe, which received considerable critical acclaim and an Academy Award nomination.

The Lord of the Rings Trilogy offered Astin the opportunity to take on a role that was unlike any he had played previously: 'You have got these characters who are facing larger than life obstacles; innocent, little, big-footed people who are in way over their heads. Except that I don't think the hobbits see themselves as being "little" until they are standing next to something that's daunting and intimidating. So I've tried to approach the character as being as real and human as possible.

Sam begins his journey as Frodo's manservant. He comes from a lower class and is not so well educated as his master. However, as the adventure unfolds, their relationship deepens into one of love and mutual dependence: 'To me there is nothing so admirable as a passionate love-bond between two human beings. Sam loves Frodo and wants to protect him and Frodo is extremely protective of Sam. So what you have are these two people locked into this journey together. They don't need to explain what they are to each other; they don't need to talk about it; they just *are*.'

Summing up his approach to the role of Sam, Sean Astin says: 'I just wanted to allow whatever essence of goodness there is within me to come forth and to inhabit the role of Sam, because that's what he is: he's goodness, loyalty, decency; that, I think, is his function in the books.'

sean Bean
BOROMIR

'Because Boromir is a man, as opposed to an Elf, Dwarf or hobbit, he brings, I think, a very human quality to the Fellowship.' Sean Bean is considering his character in *The Lord of the Rings Trilogy*.

The role is a complex one: Boromir is the eldest son of Denethor, Steward of Gondor, the southern realm of Middle-earth, which is being beleaguered by the forces of the Dark Lord Sauron. Having travelled to Rivendell to speak at the Council of Elrond on behalf of his people, Boromir becomes a member of the Fellowship.

Though noble and heroic, Boromir has a fatal flaw: 'Being human,' says Bean, 'he's more susceptible to the power of the Ring and is constantly having to fight against it. He knows that it's got a strong draw on him and, throughout the journey, that keeps preying on his mind.'

Boromir's fascination with the Ring places the entire quest in peril. As Bean remarks: 'By the end, although it is too late, he understands why it's just not possible to take the Ring and use it.'

With his recent film and television work, the British-born actor has gained two distinct reputations for himself: as the hard man and the lover. As well as playing Alec Trevelyan (006) the good-guy-turned-bad-guy who opposes Pierce Brosnan's Bond in *Goldeneye* and Sean Miller, the terrorist who pursues Harrison Ford in *Patriot Games*, Bean has shown a more romantic side to his personality as the compromised photographer in *A Woman's Guide to Adultery* and as Mellors, the gamekeeper lover in *Lady Chatterley*, Ken Russell's TV adaptation of D H Lawrence's infamous novel.

After studying at the Royal Academy of Dramatic Art, Bean began his stage career in London's West End in a variety of Shakespearean roles before making his film debut in *Caravaggio*. Other films include *War Requiem*, *Black Beauty* and the Robert De Niro spy-thriller, *Ronin*, in which he plays the role of Spence, the British weapons expert. On television, Sean has starred in a number of popular series, among them *Lorna Doone*, *Clarissa*, *Scarlett* and his acclaimed performance in the title-role of *Sharpe*, the Napoleonic war hero in the novels of Bernard Cornwell.

A diverse and talented actor, Bean's recent work has ranged from the gangster Jason Locke in *Essex Boys* to providing the voice for the Nun's Priest in an award-winning puppet version of *The Canterbury Tales*.

Bean's role in *The Lord of the Rings* is both phyically and emotionally demanding: grappling with a character who acts quite wrongly for many of the best motives. Sean Bean describes Boromir as 'Resolute, determined and clear thinking; a man of battle, Boromir has a very clear opinion about wanting to use the Ring to help his people. But although he has very direct ambitions, he eventually comes to see things in a different light.'

cate Blanchett
Galadriel

'**I**t sounds ridiculous,' jokes Cate Blanchett, 'but one of the reasons I wanted to play Galadriel was for the ears: I've *always* wanted pointy ears!'

Blanchett, the actress who won a Golden Globe and Bafta Awards and received an Oscar nomination for her portrayal of Queen Elizabeth I of England, is cast in *The Lord of the Rings Trilogy* as Galadriel, the beautiful queen of the Elves, who gives gifts and counsel to the Fellowship of the Ring when they come to her city in the Golden Wood of Lothlórien.

Galadriel – whose name, in translation, means 'Lady of Light' – is a character of power and wisdom. 'She is very mercurial,' says Blanchett. There is a sadness about her that comes from her knowledge that the age of the Elves in Middle-earth is coming to an end, but there is also an edge of danger to her character because she, too, is a ring-bearer and has the potential – were she to take the One Ring – to become a force as terrible as the Dark Lord Sauron himself.'

Within a year of graduating from Australia's National Institute of Dramatic Art, Blanchett was receiving critical praise for her theatrical performances in plays by David Mamet and Caryl Churchill. Blanchett made her feature film debut as a member of a strong female cast headed by Glenn Close in *Paradise Road*, a film about a group of women imprisoned in Sumatra by the Japanese during World War II.

Her second film, *Thank God He Met Lizzie* won her the Australian Film Critic's Circle award and the Afi Awards for Best Supporting Actress and was followed by *Oscar* and *Lucinda*, co-starring with Ralph Fiennes, and her acclaimed performance in the title-role of *Elizabeth*.

Subsequent films have included a film version of Oscar Wilde's *An Ideal Husband*, *The Talented Mr Ripley*, *Pushing Tin*, and *A man Who Cried*. Most Recently, she starred in *The Gift*, directed by Sam Raimi.

The invitation to play Galadriel was one that Blanchett was eager to accept: 'I love the book, I wanted to work with Peter Jackson and I was interested in being part of a story that had a fantastical element to it, but which was being told in a way that was absolutely "real".'

Since filming her scenes for *The Lord of the Rings*, Blanchett has played the heroine of *Charlotte Gray*, as well as completing *Bandits* along side Bruce Willis and Billy Bob Thornton, *Heaven* co-staring Gioranai Ribisi, and *The Shipping News* with Kevin Spacey.

Reflecting on the film adaptation of J R R Tolkien's *The Lord of the Rings*, Blanchett observes: 'This book has had a powerful influence on people for almost fifty years and to have had the opportunity to work on these films has been a privilege: as if we were handing on the torch of our admiration for this book to generations to come.'

ORLANDO BLOOM
Legolas

'When I think of Legolas,' says Orlando Bloom, 'I think of a cat. You know how a cat will hop up on a table and just suddenly stop with no forward motion, staying absolutely still and alert? Cats never look stiff or heavy, they are graceful and poised, but always switched-on. That's Legolas.'

Bloom decided that he wanted to act when he was still a schoolboy: 'There was a girl in my class whom all the guys had a crush on. We used to run races in the playground at lunchtime to see who would be her boyfriend for the day! I had always loved watching *Superman* on television and I used to fantasize that I could just fly in, pick up the girl and zoom off again!' He laughs and adds, 'At the same time, of course, I realized that a character like *Superman* was just an actor playing the part and it was about that time that I thought: *that* is the job for me.'

At the age of sixteen Bloom spent two seasons with the National Youth Theatre and by the time he began his training at London's Guildhall School of Music and Drama – where he performed in productions such as *Peer Gynt*, *Twelfth Night*, *The Seagull* and *Antigone* – he had already made his film debut in *Wilde*, as one of the working-class lads who caught the eye of the famous playwright, Oscar Wilde. Following this, Bloom performed in the television series, *Midsomer Murders*.

Still at drama school when he attended an audition for *The Lord of the Rings*, Bloom originally read for the part of Boromir's brother, Faramir, who is introduced in *The Two Towers*. Since there were a lot of young actors auditioning and he was busy with his studies, Bloom didn't give a lot of thought to how he had fared: 'I suppose it was lucky that I didn't, because I might have got overwhelmed by the idea.'

After waiting six months Bloom heard that although he had not been cast as Faramir, he was being asked to audition again for Legolas: 'I thought: "Definitely! Game on!" So I learned the scene and acted it on video tape and, shortly after, got this incredible phone call saying that they were offering me the role! It was like winning the lottery! Like having all your dreams fulfilled! It was amazing!'

Having secured the role of Legolas, Bloom rapidly became expert on the ways of Elves: 'They are the first-born, the oldest and the wisest of the races in Middle-earth. They are ageless and immortal. They have never known sickness or pestilence. They can be slain in battle or die of a broken heart – but, otherwise, that's about it! Tolkien's Elves are nothing like the traditional image of pixies and fairies: they have great physical and mental strength and are powerful, full-blooded people.'

'As for Legolas,' adds Orlando Bloom, 'he has seen the world. He is incredibly experienced in many ways. Mind you, so he *should* be – after all, he *is* 2,931 years old!'

BILLY BOYD
PIPPIN

'Pippin is an individual, he has a lot of spontaneity. He also sees life from a slightly different angle to most people.' So too, does Scottish actor, Billy Boyd, cast in the role of Peregrin Took, affectionately known to everyone as 'Pippin'.

A close friend of Frodo Baggins and his cousin, Merry, Pippin helps the Ring-bearer on his flight from the Shire and is then chosen to be a member of the Fellowship of the Ring.

'Although Pippin has never left the Shire,' says Billy Boyd, 'he is a Took and comes from a family that is known for being a bit adventurous and likely to fly off the handle and do things that other hobbits would consider to be not quite hobbit-like! What's more, Pippin does have a habit of doing the wrong things at the wrong time! Although, to be fair, as the story develops, we see Pippin going through all kinds of experiences and becoming more mature.'

Born in Glasgow, Scotland, Billy Boyd is a musician as well as an actor, playing bass, drums and guitar and singing both baritone and tenor. He began his acting career in the theatre and is well established as one of Scotland's leading talents. His first television role was in the popular Scottish television series, *Taggart*.

Boyd made his film debut playing a loan shark in the Jason Connery movie, *Urban Ghost Story* and was then cast for *The Lord of the Rings Trilogy*.

'I liked Peter Jackson the moment I met him,' he recalls, 'he was just so laid back. We were in a casting agent's office and there was Peter – dressed, as usual, in shorts and without shoes – sitting on a sofa with Fran Walsh. They were both so relaxed with me, that it was easy to be relaxed with them and to be open about what I wanted to bring to the character of Pippin.'

One of the topics the director discussed with the young actor at his audition was the close relationship between Pippin and Merry. 'It's not really possible,' says Billy Boyd, 'to speak about Pippin without mentioning Merry: his whole life revolves around his friends and Merry in particular. They are just like the closest of friends so that you really can't imagine either of them doing anything without the other.'

Ian Holm
BILBO

'**B**ilbo is not unlike me. My grandchildren call me "Grumpy". Not "Grampy", but "*Grumpy*"! I've even got a Grumpy T-shirt! And I think Bilbo is quite grumpy, too – although, of course, he has a heart of gold.'

Sir Ian Holm is talking about his role as Bilbo Baggins, Frodo's 'uncle', who, many years earlier had come into possession of the One Ring. J R R Tolkien recounted Bilbo's exploits in *The Hobbit* and *The Lord of the Rings* opens with Bilbo leaving his home in Hobbiton on another journey. In going, he makes Frodo his heir bequeathing him all his possessions – including the Ring.

Appearing in *The Lord of the Rings Trilogy* is a return to Middle-earth for Holm who, twenty-one years ago, starred as Frodo in an acclaimed BBC radio serialisation of Tolkien's epic. Reflecting on the character he once played (now being portrayed by Elijah Wood) he observes: 'Frodo is an extraordinary fellow: like Bilbo, he is only a little chap, but, somehow, his indomitable spirit keeps him going.'

Holm's involvement with Tolkien's classic is just one of a number of associations with 'literary fantasies': he portrayed J M Barrie, the creator of Peter Pan, in the award-winning television drama series, *The Lost Boys*, and Lewis Carroll, the author of *Alice in Wonderland* in the film *Dreamchild*.

An illustrious stage career began with an appearance as 'a spear-carrier' in a production of *Othello*. A decade later, his performance as Henry V, in one of numerous productions with the Royal Shakespeare Company, earned him the *Evening Standard* 'Best Actor' award, as did his performance, the following year, in Harold Pinter's *The Homecoming*, the Broadway production of which won him a Tony Award.

Holm began making films in the 1960s and had his first notable role in *The Fixer* starring Alan Bates and Dirk Bogarde. After a number of historical pictures (*Mary, Queen of Scots* and *Young Winston*), he played *Nostromo* crew-member Ash in *Alien* and gained an Academy Award nomination for his role in *Chariots of Fire*. Subsequent films include an appearance as Napoleon in *Time Bandits* and roles in *Greystoke, Brazil, Dance with a Stranger, Frankenstein* and *The Madness of King George*, which earned him his second Oscar nomination.

After a lengthy absence from the stage, Holm returned to the theatre with award-winning performances in Harold Pinter's *Moonlight* and Shakespeare's *King Lear*. Recent films have included *Night Falls on Manhattan, The Fifth Element* and *The Sweet Hereafter*.

In 1998 Holm was awarded his knighthood.

Having previously played Frodo, Sir Ian Holm enjoyed playing the older hobbit: 'Bilbo is a character to whom things seem "to happen"! But once put to his mettle, once put to the test, he comes up trumps.'

The only problem has been getting used to wearing prosthetic feet: 'I keep tripping over them and nearly falling on my face! I think my feet are bigger than anybody else's. I don't know why – I suppose because I'm Bilbo Baggins!'

CHRISTOPHER Lee

Saruman

'**I** always had this dream that, one day, somebody would make *The Lord of the Rings* into a motion picture and that I would be in it.' Christopher Lee is talking about the experience of playing a character in a book that he loves with a passion.

'I read *The Hobbit* first,' recalls Lee, 'and then I read all three volumes of *The Lord of the Rings*, as they were published. I was completely bowled over by them: the imagination behind the work is wonderful. Every year ever since then I have re-read the book and I still think it's one of the great works of literature, certainly of this past century, possibly of all time.'

Christopher Lee plays the wizard Saruman the White: once the greatest and wisest of the order to which he and Gandalf belong, but who has been corrupted by the power of the Dark Lord Sauron. 'There have been many Sarumans in my lifetime.' says Lee. 'Men of genius, intellect and power who went wrong. And, in opposition to Saruman the White, Tolkien places Gandalf the Grey: two sides of the same coin. Here you have the universal conflict between good and evil and the powers behind those two elements: and that will have a relevance for every audience, everywhere – because we all know, or have heard of, such people and conflicts in *our* world.'

Having appeared in some two hundred and fifty-five films and television productions, Lee has the distinction of being listed in *The Guinness Book of Movie Facts and Feats* as the international star with the most screen credits. Numbered among those credits are the many sinister roles which Lee created for Hammer, the British production company which in the 1950s revived the public's fascination with 'horror movies'. In playing both Frankenstein's 'Creature' and Dracula, Lee became the successor to 30s movie legends Boris Karloff and Bela Lugosi.

Although best-known for his horror roles – Christopher Lee also portrayed Rasputin, Fu Manchu and the Mummy – he has played a diversity of roles in many languages (among them English, Russian, French and Italian): he was Conan Doyle's famous detective in the German-made picture, *Sherlock Holmes and the Deadly Necklace*, and later played Holmes' brother, Mycroft, in Billy Wilder's *The Private Life of Sherlock Holmes*.

Among Lee's 'rogues' gallery' are the Marquis St Evremonde in *A Tale of Two Cities* and Rochefort in the 70s productions of *The Three* (and *Four*) *Musketeers*. He was also Lord Summerisle, the leader of the pagan cult, in *The Wicker Man*; Dr Catheter, the medical genius behind the Splice of Life laboratory responsible for the 'new batch' of nasties let loose in *Gremlins II*; and the evil Francisco Scaramanga, James Bond's title-opponent in *The Man with the Golden Gun*.

Christopher Lee continues to demonstrate his extraordinary versatility in film roles that range from his inter-galactic appearance as Count Dooku/Darth Tyranus in *Star Wars: Episode II* to his portrayal of Mohammed Ali Jinnah, the founder of modern Pakistan, in the 1998 film, *Jinnah*.

As for Christopher Lee's casting as Saruman, this remains an especial delight in a long and impressive career: 'Although I always hoped that this film would one day be made, it is a mighty saga, a huge canvas, and I always supposed that it would prove too daunting for any director. Then Peter Jackson undertook the task, asked me to play Saruman and my dream came true!'

IAN MCKELLEN
Gandalf

'**G**andalf is not just a creation of Tolkien, he is *the* wizard, the prototype of wizards. He looks like how we expect a wizard to look.'

Dressed in grey robes and sporting a grey beard and a false nose, Sir Ian McKellen reflects on the character of Gandalf and his kinship with various magical figures in literature: 'Tolkien was playing with various types of character: the wizard from fairy-stories, Merlin in the Arthurian legends, maybe even Prospero in Shakespeare's play, *The Tempest*.'

Known in Elvish as Mithrandir ('Grey-wanderer'), Gandalf is one of the chief wizards, or Istari, of Middle-earth. A friend to Bilbo Baggins and his nephew, Frodo, Gandalf knows something of the dark history and fearful destiny bound up in the One Ring and has a crucial part to play in the struggle against the Lord of the Rings.

When he embarked on the role of Gandalf, McKellen received many suggestions as to how he should play the character: 'From teenagers and readers old as wizards came the advice, the demands, the warnings – united by the hope that the film's Gandalf would match their own individual interpretations.'

The actor is philosophic about meeting the expectations of the books' admirers: 'I can't be everybody's Gandalf, I have to be the Gandalf that belongs in this particular movie and he comes out of myself, out of the script and out of my response to it. If that Gandalf happens to accord with other people's Gandalf, I shall be delighted.'

After studying at Cambridge University, but without any formal training, McKellen made his professional debut in a production of *A Man for all Seasons*. It was the beginning of a distinguished stage career during which he has given memorable performances in many Shakespearean roles as well as starring in powerful contemporary dramas such as *Bent* and *Amadeus*. His first film role, opposite Gregory Peck, was in the unfinished, 1966 picture, *The Bells of Hell go Ting-a-ling-a-ling*.

Subsequently, he portrayed novelist D H Lawrence in the film *Priest of Love*; Tsar Nicholas II in *Rasputin* (for which he won a Golden Globe Award); and film-maker James Whale (the director of *Frankenstein*) in *Gods and Monsters*.

McKellen's other films include *Apt Pupil*, *Restoration*, *Six Degrees of Separation*, *Plenty* and *X-Men* as well as co-writing, executive producing and starring in his award-winning modern-dress production of *Richard III*.

Sitting in the make-up chair each morning at 4.30, Sir Ian McKellen ponders the necessity for beards, wigs – and false noses. 'Of course,' he laughs, 'I really have to look like everyone's idea of a wizard and if it means making my nose bigger then so be it!' He pauses and then, with a twinkle in his eye, remarks: 'Actually, I suspect that Gandalf *does* wear a false nose – and a wig – and that he has a quite different persona at the other end of the forest!'

DOMINIC MONAGHAN
merry

'When the story begins,' explains Dominic Monaghan, 'Merry is in the prime of life, he's having fun and he's well liked. He's really just one of the lads. Then, as the journey unfolds, he finds himself in situations where he has to look after people or make decisions that a hobbit would never normally have to make.'

Monaghan plays Merry (full name: Meriadoc Brandybuck), second cousin and childhood companion of Frodo Baggins. It is Merry, along with Pippin and Sam, who helps Frodo when he first sets out on his dangerous journey, during which he becomes part of the Fellowship of the Ring and has many adventures before the story and the quest reach their dramatic conclusion.

Describing his character (and that of Pippin), Monaghan says: 'Merry and Pippin come across as vibrant characters. Frodo is weighed down by the mission he's got to undertake and Sam is terribly serious about doing his job, but these two are really the wild cards in the pack and the spice in the Fellowship.'

Monaghan (who at 5' 7" is 'officially the tallest hobbit'), went directly from his sixth form college in Cheshire to work in youth theatres in Manchester. Spotted by an agent, he was given the role of Geoffrey Shawcross in the BBC television series *Hetty Wainthropp Investigates*. Playing the juvenile sidekick to the doughty senior-citizen detective, portrayed by Patricia Routledge, led to other television roles, a film debut alongside Rutger Hauer and Martin Sheen in *Boomber*, and an invitation to audition for *The Lord of the Rings*.

He was already an admirer of Tolkien's books to which he had been introduced by his school teacher father: 'My dad's a big fan of Tolkien. He used to go on and on about what a great book *The Hobbit* was and how Bilbo Baggins was such a fantastic character. Once I'd read *The Hobbit*, he gave me *The Lord of the Rings*, saying that it was a challenge, but was well worth reading. He was right: it is a challenge, because it's so big and huge and vast, but it's *well* worth it!'

'Auditioning for *The Lord of the Rings*,' recalls Monaghan, 'I was really excited and really nervous!' Monaghan was rehearsing for a play in London when he was invited to audition for the film. For him, the project was the Holy Grail. While trying to calm himself down about potentially being involved, Monaghan landed a lead role in *Monsignor Renard* in France, starring John Thaw.

Nearly six months later, he was offered the part of Merry, a role with which he feels particularly at ease: 'I think that Merry is well-known in the Shire: he's charming and cheeky and I imagine that all the hobbit mothers probably pretend to be annoyed by him, but really like him!' Which is something he has experienced a great deal while growing up!

VIGGO MORTENSEN
ARAGORN

'What is Aragorn like?' Viggo Mortensen asks rhetorically. 'He is someone who is self-reliant and a little reclusive.' It is tempting to see parallels between the player and the role: Mortensen is perfectly content to spend days with just his own company and admits to being happier among trees than around people.

Born in Manhattan, New York, Mortensen's family travelled extensively, living in Venezuela, Argentina and Denmark (his father is Danish) so that, by an early age, he and his two younger brothers had developed a knack for adapting to new and different surroundings. He feels a particular affinity, therefore, with the character of Aragorn, who, in the book, is first encountered in the guise of a wandering Ranger known as 'Strider'.

Mortensen's role in *The Lord of the Rings Trilogy* is complex and demanding: when Frodo first meets him at the Prancing Pony Inn at Bree, he is a mysterious, seemingly sinister figure who seems to knows an alarming amount about Mr Baggins and the mission that is taking him out of the Shire. As the story unfolds, however, 'Strider' is revealed to be Aragorn II, the uncrowned king of the race of men in Middle-earth. The fate of the Ring-bearer, it becomes clear, is inextricably linked to Aragorn's own destiny.

The actor has indicated that he identifies easily with characters who find themselves set apart from those around them as Aragorn does. However, in a career spanning more than thirty films, Mortensen has played a wide range of roles, from the romantic suitors of Nicole Kidman in *Portrait of a Lady* and Diane Lane in *A Walk on the Moon*, to an assortment of villains and hard men.

Early performances by Mortensen in films by Jonathan Demme and Woody Allen ended up on the cutting room floor, but his eventual debut in Peter Weir's *Witness* created an immediate awareness of his acting talent and, over the ensuing years, he came to be seen in such diverse films as *The Indian Runner, Boiling Point, The Prophecy, Carlito's Way, G.I. Jane, A Perfect Murder* and *Psycho.*

Although few cinema audiences would have been aware of the fact, all the paintings and photographs seen on the set for the artist's studio in *A Perfect Murder* were by Mortensen himself. It is scarcely surprising that the actor is now frequently referred to as a Renaissance Man, since not only is he a painter, but also a published poet, whose multimedia books and CDs include *Ten Last Night, Recent Forgeries* and *The Other Parade.*

Viggo Mortensen approached the role of Aragorn both as an actor who responds to physical challenges, welcoming the opportunity to do his own riding and fighting, and as a poet, reacting to the symbolism in Tolkien's myth: 'Aragorn is deeply aware of the burden of his heritage and he carries the knowledge that, all too soon, he will have to reveal his true self in order to play his part in the fight against Sauron. That burden, that knowledge is what shapes and colours his perceptions.'

JOHN RHYS-DAVIES
GIMLI

'**D**o you want to know why I got involved in this?' asks John Rhys-Davies. 'I really wanted to play a character called Denethor. He is Boromir's father and doesn't appear until *The Two Towers*. I thought: I can go to New Zealand for a few weeks, be in one or two wonderful scenes and go home knowing that I was in one of the biggest pictures of all time. That was the idea!'

However, like several cast members of *The Lord of the Rings Trilogy*, John Rhys-Davies did not get his first-choice role: 'I was totally shaken when they came back and asked me to play Gimli!'

Undertaking the role of Gimli was to prove a challenge, not least because of the many hours spent in the make-up department undergoing the daily transformation of his features into those of a Dwarf. Despite the discomfort of wearing a quantity of prosthetic make-up (to which Rhys-Davies' skin developed an allergic reaction), the actor quickly became aware of the character's importance within the Fellowship of the Ring and the dramatic structure of the saga.

'There is,' explains Rhys-Davies, 'an energetic ferocity in the Dwarf that the film needs. It's often these minor characters who really have to impart a sense of energy and dynamism to a film so that the heroes can actually take their time to respond and be thoughtful and reflective.'

It is something that the Welsh-born actor well understands, having played several such film parts, including his memorable appearances as Harrison Ford's roguish sidekick, Sallah, in *Raiders of the Lost Ark* and *Indiana Jones and the Last Crusade*.

Rhys-Davies studied at London's Royal Academy of Dramatic Art and in addition to his distinguished theatre work – Othello, Macbeth and Falstaff – has taken leading roles in many movies, among them *Victor/Victoria*, *The Living Daylights*, *King Solomon's Mines* and the 1992 re-make of Conan Doyle's *The Lost World* in which he starred as Professor Challenger.

His prolific television-credits include playing Vasco Rodrigues in James Clavell's *Shogun*, Agent Malone in the British series, *The Untouchables* and Joe Gargery in Charles Dickens' *Great Expectations*. Rhys-Davies has also starred in the TV mini-series, *War and Remembrance* and has made guest appearances in *Murder, She Wrote* and *Star Trek: Voyager*, in which he has twice portrayed Leonardo da Vinci!

Reflecting on Tolkien's story and the decision to film it in New Zealand with Peter Jackson as director, Rhys-Davies says: 'In the twilight of gloom, darkness and evil that is encompassing and about to overthrow the world, there are still men of virtue, there is still humour, honour, courage and compassion. And we couldn't have picked a better director or a better country to encapsulate that drama.'

And as for the dwarf: 'Well,' laughs John Rhys-Davies, 'Gimli is a short fellow, so it was really very interesting: I've never played a part before where I had to look up all the time I was acting!'

Liv Tyler
Arwen

Liv Tyler, an actress who has been described as 'cool' and 'beguiling' with 'dazzling eyes' and 'flawless porcelain skin', is cast as the Lady Arwen, the beautiful daughter of Elrond, the Lord of Rivendell.

Known among her people as 'Evenstar', it is Arwen's deep love for Aragorn that sustains the heroic warrior through the desperate struggles of the War of the Ring and which will bring her, at last, to make a terrible choice: whether to pass into the Undying Lands of the West with her father and the other Elven folk, or to remain with Aragorn in Middle-earth where she would become of mortal kind and eventually die.

It is fitting that the role of Arwen should go to an actress now ranked amongst the leading beauties of contemporary cinema. Making her debut in Bruce Beresford's *Silent Fall*, Liv Tyler played leading roles in films such as *Empire Records* and *Heavy*, before receiving critical attention, in 1996, for her performance in *Stealing Beauty* from the Italian director, Bernardo Bertolucci, a film that had cinema commentators comparing her with the young Elizabeth Taylor to the extent of briefly re-naming her 'Liv Taylor'.

After a successful appearance in Tom Hank's directorial debut, *That Thing You Do!*, Tyler co-starred with Bruce Willis and Ben Affleck in *Armageddon*, a film that won her roles in Robert Altman's *Cookie's Fortune*, in the period romance-romp *Plunkett & Macleane* and opposite Ralph Fiennes in the film of Alexander Pushkin's *Onegin*. She recently appeared in *One Night at McCool's* opposite Matt Dillon, and was reunited with Robert Altman when she starred in the critically acclaimed *Dr. T and the Women* with Richard Gere.

Tyler is very conscious of starring in a film dominated by male characters: 'I see it as an honour to be one of only a few women in the picture and to bring the feminine touch to the story.'

Arwen, however, is an unconventional woman and her love-affair with Aragorn is set against the threatening backdrop of war. 'So she has to be patient and supportive and let him go off and do the things that he has to do. But she is impatient, too. When you're in love, you want to spend all your time with that person, and she finds it difficult that they can't be together.'

Born in New York and raised in Portland, Maine, prior to returning to Manhattan, Liv Tyler was required to adopt an English accent for the role of Arwen. She also had learn to speak in Elvish and move as an Elf maiden might: 'I had to carry myself in a certain way and be aware of my breathing. It was a challenge for me as an American speaking in a British accent, but as an Elf I had to be so erect and centred and to move effortlessly and gracefully.'

HUGO WEAVING
eLROND

'Having agreed to play Elrond,' says Hugo Weaving, 'I realized how much had to be worked out about this character: the idea of portraying someone who is immortal, for one thing; plus the fact that he is noble, wise, powerful, good – and beautiful! I began to think that he was altogether impossible to play!'

Although it was the role of the humanoid, Agent Smith, in the American special-effects bonanza, *The Matrix*, that brought Hugo Weaving international fame, he was already well-established in his homeland, Australia, as a star of film, television and theatre.

Born in Nigeria, Weaving lived in South Africa and England before moving with his family to Sydney, Australia. On leaving school he trained at the National Institute of Dramatic Art and, within a few years, was cast in a TV mini-series, *Bodyline*, playing the central role of the controversial British cricketer, Douglas Jardine.

Weaving's television career continued with *Bangkok Hilton*, starring alongside Nicole Kidman. In addition to his TV work and a number of challenging stage roles, Weaving was giving award-winning performances in a string of acclaimed films.

Proof, the story of a blind man who insists on taking photographs as 'proof' that the world is as others describe it to him, won him the Australian Film Institute 'Best Actor Award', as did his performance in *The Interview*. This acclaimed movie about a man undergoing a gruelling police interrogation also won Weaving a Film Critics Circle of Australia nomination and the Best Actor Award at the World Film Festival in Montreal.

Weaving received a further AFI nomination for Best Actor for his portrayal of the drag-artiste, Mitzi, in *The Adventures of Priscilla, Queen of the Desert*. Teetering on twelve-inch high stilettos, Weaving and his co-stars Guy Pearce and Terence Stamp won the hearts of cinema-goers in Australia and Europe and, whilst Hollywood remade *Priscilla* with American 'names', audiences in the United States were soon to discover Weaving's acting talents when he assumed the role of Keanu Reeves' nemesis in *The Matrix*. The executive producer of *The Matrix* was Barrie Osborne who went on to become producer of *The Lord of the Rings Trilogy*.

Returning to the difficulties of playing an Elf with immortality, Hugo Weaving says: 'Elrond is a fount of knowledge and wisdom: he knows a great deal about the history of the Ring and understands not just what *has* happened, but what *might* happen. Elrond is well aware that whether the Ring is destroyed or taken by Sauron, the time of the Elves is almost at an end. Whatever the outcome, the Elves will leave Middle-earth and be forgotten. There is, therefore, a sadness about Elrond which made me decide that – although he is an Elf – he also needed to have humanity, and that is what I have tried to bring to my performance.'

eLijah wood
frodo

'This is the first time I've played a fifty-year-old!' notes Elijah Wood with a laugh. He is, after all, only just twenty! Wood plays Frodo Baggins, the hobbit who inherits a magic ring with the alarming consequence that he has to set out on a terror-filled journey towards the shadow-filled land of Mordor. 'According to the book,' continues Wood, 'Frodo is fifty when he sets out on his quest, although fifty is still relatively young in the life-span of a hobbit. And this particular hobbit is fascinating.'

Frodo is the nephew of Bilbo Baggins, and Wood sees a similarity between those two characters: 'Frodo is different, he is slightly set apart from the other hobbits. Like his uncle, he is very curious about the outside world. Frodo has read Bilbo's memoirs and heard the older hobbit telling stories of his adventures, and part of him likes the idea of having an adventure of his own.'

When, however, that adventure comes to Frodo, it turns out to be a lot more dangerous than he, or his uncle, might have anticipated. His task is to carry the One Ring into Mordor, avoiding the watchful gaze of the Dark Lord, Sauron, and there cast the Ring into the fires of Mount Doom.

The Lord of the Rings Trilogy is the latest venture for an actor who has already achieved much in his tender years. Following early success as a child model, Wood's family moved to Los Angeles. It was there that an agent saw Wood and asked if he would like to be an actor. 'Why not?' answered Wood and he was soon launched on his film career with minor roles in *Back to the Future II*, *Internal Affairs* and *Avalon*.

His first starring role, at the age of ten, was in *Paradise*, playing Willard, a young boy who re-awakens the love between Melanie Griffith and Don Johnson as a couple whose lives have been devastated by a family tragedy. Later films include *Forever Young, The Good Son, North, Flipper, The Ice Storm, Deep Impact, Chain of Fools* and *The Faculty*. In 1994 Wood was named Young Star of the Year by NATO/ShowEast following his performance in *The War*.

Wood has also portrayed two famous literary characters, one American and one English: starring in the title role of Mark Twain's *The Adventures of Huckleberry Finn* and playing the Artful Dodger, opposite Richard Dreyfuss as Fagin, in a television version of Charles Dickens' *Oliver Twist*.

In playing Frodo, Wood is cast alongside fellow American Sean Astin as Sam Gamgee. As Wood observes, the special bond that grows and develops between Frodo and Sam in the three volumes of the book is also at the heart of the film trilogy: 'It is a deep relationship and difficult to describe. In one way it is a master/servant relationship because Sam comes from a different class and wants to serve Frodo and be there for him because he's very, very loyal. But, more than anything, they are best friends.'

Despite all the efforts of wizards and warriors, it is this one friendship that eventually enables Frodo to carry out his quest: 'Quite simply, it is love,' says Elijah Wood. 'It is that unconditional love that says, regardless of what you do or where you go, I will always be there for you.'

marton csokas
celeborn

Born in New Zealand, Marton Csokas's film credits include *The Monkey's Mask*, *Broken English*, *Down and Under*, *Rain* and *Star Wars: Episode II*. For television, Csokas has performed in a range of dramas including *The Three Stooges*, *Xena*, *G.P.* (for which he received an Australian Film Institute nomination), *Farscape*, *Halifax f.p.* and *Wildside*.

A graduate of the New Zealand Drama School, Csokas's performances on stage include New Zealand productions of *Arcadia*, *Angels in America*, *Julius Caesar*, *Glorious Ruins*, *Amy's View* and *Closer*. In Australia, Csokas has performed on the stage in *A Clockwork Orange*, *Twelfth Night*, *The Herbal Bed* and *Andromache* as well as an Australian tour of *Ladies' Night*.

Csokas also co-founded the Stronghold Theatre in Australasia, which has created such pieces as *Possibilities*, *Meeting Place* and *Media Sluts*, all of which played to great acclaim.

fantasy to reality

'The settings in Tolkien's books are not backgrounds: they are very much a part of the story.'

SUPERVISING ART DIRECTOR DAN HENNAH

Creating the diversity of settings for *The Lord of the Rings* has been a challenge to the film-makers. 'It is,' says Dan Hennah, 'a bit like a "road-movie": everywhere is different, a new place, with its own particular spirit.' Beginning with the rural tranquillity of Hobbiton in the Shire, from where the adventure begins, the central characters journey to the towns and cities of men, the ancient strongholds of Elves and Dwarves. Each place has a distinct and individual character and significantly affects the events in the story.

The scenes filmed in Hobbiton not only help establish the personality of Frodo and the other hobbits, they offer somewhere – comfortable and reassuring – by which all the other places visited, whether beautiful or threatening, may be assessed.

The first of these places is Bree, the town of men where Frodo expects to meet with Gandalf. As Sean Astin, playing Sam, observes: 'It is in Bree that, for the first time, the hobbits really have a sense of having gone beyond a place of safety and ventured on an adventure that is perilous.'

The aim of the film's Art Department, says Dan Hennah, was to create an unsettling atmosphere in Bree: 'The people of Bree are just normal people. But they are all much bigger than the hobbits so they feel threatening. We worked on making everything tall, thin and slightly out of true line, so the buildings feel as though they are looming in over you just as all the humans are towering over the hobbits as they walk through the streets.'

Merry in the Prancing Pony Inn

When the hobbits enter the Prancing Pony Inn in Bree they are surrounded by the tables and chairs – and people – that, to them, seem huge. 'All of a sudden,' says Sean Astin, 'the hobbits are confronted by gritty, tense-looking people and, for the first time, they are unable to look anybody in the eye. It is a real "We're not in Kansas any more, Toto" moment!'

In contrast to Bree, Rivendell – home of the Elven lord, Elrond – is a place of peace and beauty. 'I think Rivendell is a good example of somewhere that feels real but is also totally unlike anywhere that anyone has ever been before,' says Alan Lee. 'Because the Elves live in very close harmony with nature, the buildings are constructed with openings to allow room for the surrounding trees to grow. It's all very light and open; there's no glass in the windows, there are drifts of leaves in the interiors and all that separates the inside from the outside is a screen of fine filigree woodwork.'

Preparations for building Rivendell began eighteen months before the start of filming, with the planting of trees and vines that would eventually be incorporated into a landscape that includes wooded glades and artificially-constructed waterfalls. Waterfalls need rocks and, unlikely though it sounds, those in Rivendell were made from foam, under the supervision of Weta Workshop's Rock and Foam Department Supervisor Nick Williams. While making fake rocks might sound simple, co-ordinating the various stages so that the end-product looked right was more complex. The fake rocks might be used on a studio set that needed to have continuity with outdoor shots, filmed on location; while others might be used at an exterior set where it was essential that they merge with the surrounding environment. 'In the end,' says Nick Williams, 'it's got to look good. If it doesn't look good, it's not right, and if it's not right it's not happening!'

For the cast, walking onto the Rivendell set for the first time, with peacocks strutting to and fro, was a revelation.

'It was just mind-blowing,' says Orlando Bloom, playing Legolas, the Elven prince who becomes part of the story at Rivendell. 'It's just as I imagined it would be, if I could have pictured it that clearly. The Elves have, and make, more beauty than any other earthly creatures, and Rivendell is the epicentre of that beauty.'

Sean Astin reflects on the often curious correlation between the shooting schedule on the film and the adventures that the hobbits go through in the books: 'By the time we got ready to film the sequences at Rivendell, we had already been through a great deal and so, all of a sudden, to be able to walk onto a set that was this paradise, this Garden of Eden, was a really wonderful escape and a welcome change from what we had previously been filming. For Frodo, Sam, Merry and Pippin and the rest of the Fellowship, it was almost as if no acting was really required: you entered this tranquil, lush, beautiful environment and simply created this feeling of peace within yourself.'

Beyond Rivendell, the Fellowship travel through many other extraordinary places, each of which has been recreated by the film-makers with amazing sets and breathtaking locations, including the snow-swept slopes of Caradhras, the dark labyrinthine passageways of the Mines of Moria and the Golden Wood of Lothlórien.

And beyond these, yet more regions – forests, plains and wastelands, with their castles and cities – that will not be seen by cinema-goers until the release of *The Two Towers* and *The Return of the King*.

Frodo's room in Rivendell

'*Well, here I am in Middle-earth, having just arrived from England, via Los Angeles!*' Wigged, bearded, cloaked and hatted, Sir Ian McKellen is sitting on an old cart ready to film the wizard's arrival in Hobbiton in time for Bilbo Baggins' eleventy-first birthday party. With a chuckle, McKellen adds: '*You know, Gandalf certainly gets around!*'

The rutted country track he is about to drive along is very narrow, hardly wide enough for the cart, which is just as it should be. For this lane leads to Hobbiton, the little rural community in that part of Middle-earth known as the Shire where the hobbits live a simple, peaceful life. The lane is hobbit-size, Gandalf's cart is human-sized, hence the tight fit! Everything else at this location in Hamilton, a few hours north of Wellington, has been constructed to the same hobbit-scale and looks amazingly authentic.

'What an introduction to working on the film this has

turned out to be,' says McKellen. 'This is a most magical place! An enchanting little gaggle of hobbit children with furry feet scampering about in an idyllic landscape that might be Oxfordshire – but which is *not* Oxfordshire – with rolling hills, dotted with the hobbit's charming little hobbit-hole homes that look as real as the trees, grass, flowers and moss that surround them. It's most thrilling!'

For Peter Jackson it was essential that Hobbiton looked as authentic as possible: 'One of the things I hate in movies is seeing a natural landscape like a garden or a lawn or a hedge where it is clear that the film's art department has gone there the day before and planted some things in pots in the ground – it just never looks real. I wanted Hobbiton to look like

hobbits have lived here for hundreds of years.'

However, as Associate Producer Rick Porras was quick to realize, this was not going to be easy: 'Every reader of the book has an image of how the place should look. I certainly had a specific picture of Hobbiton in my mind, but finding it, I thought, was going to be a tall order.'

'We set out to look for locations,' says Peter Jackson, 'and explored the country north, south, east and west before finding this little pocket of farmland near Hamilton that we thought had a really interesting hobbit-look to it.'

A large, empty field usually grazed by sheep and, in places, pretty swampy, it was not easy to see how it *could* become the Hobbiton described in Tolkien's books. Nevertheless, as Jackson walked around the farm with Conceptual Artists Alan Lee and John Howe, ideas of how the area might be modified began to take shape. 'Alan and John started drawing the landscape,' recalls Jackson, 'adding little hobbit-holes and cabbage-patches and washing-lines and hedges, literally bringing Hobbiton to life on paper. So, at that point we decided that we had found the ideal location.'

Then began the process of transformation. The first requirement was a substantial road, essential for the transportation of three to four hundred people and their equipment to the location on a daily basis. When this road had been built, with the help of the New Zealand army, the crew set to work re-landscaping the area.

An existing lake was extended and the rest of the land was drained and cleared. Major earthworks, necessitating the shifting of some five thousand kilolitres of soil, were involved in the creation of those rolling hills; fields were ploughed to look like hobbit farmland and five hundred metres of hedges were planted on the ten-acre site. Then real flowers and vegetables (cabbages, brussel sprouts and carrots) were planted in the gardens of the hobbit-holes that had been built into the sides of the hills. With filming in Hobbiton not scheduled to begin for another twelve months, all the vegetation would have a full year in which to become established before shooting began.

One tree that was planted was the massive oak which stands above Bilbo and Frodo's home at Bag End. Winched into place and secured with steel cables and concrete, its outstretched branches were then clothed in 250,000 hand-painted leaves and artificial acorns!

Bag End, with its traditional hobbit-style round doors and windows, was constructed in polystyrene, artfully painted to look as if built from stone and wood. A year's exposure to the elements, combined with some authentic-looking 'repairs', would eventually give the village the appearance of having been established for generations. 'We cut little lanes into the landscape,' remembers Peter Jackson, 'but then we allowed the weeds to grow. We spent a year just allowing Hobbiton to seed and germinate and become a *real place*.'

Arriving on location a year after construction had started, Dominic Monaghan, who plays the hobbit Merry, was struck by the significance of the world that had been created: 'I think the way in which the Shire is represented shows

the importance of the hobbits' mission from the very beginning. They set out to do what they do because they want to save this amazing place, which is like heaven on earth, with its green hills and everything blooming and the sun shining all the time and where there's no problems and no troubles. This place is really the heart of the hobbits and it's also the heart of the movie.'

'I could really happily live there the rest of my life in one of those hobbit-holes,' says Supervising Art Director Dan Hennah. *'Once you'd been in one, you just wanted to get your toothpaste and toothbrush and move in!'*

The interiors of the idiosyncratic hobbit-homes described by J R R Tolkien in his books have been lovingly visualized in the Three Foot Six studios in Wellington – and painstakingly built to match with the exteriors filmed on the Hobbiton location, where the front door of Bag End had opened not onto a fully furnished hobbit-hole but a cubbyhole big enough only to accommodate a smallish film crew.

In fact, there were *two* Bag Ends: one built for those scenes in which only the hobbits are featured, and another, meticulously scaled-down, for shots of Gandalf and the hobbits – or, to be precise, the hobbits' 'scale-doubles', the team of small actors, who, dressed identically to the full-height actors, help create the illusion that there is a significant size-difference between men and hobbits. To add yet another challenge, the smaller scale set required smaller-scale copies of all the props used in those scenes.

The interior of Bag End contains lots of tiles and polished oak (created out of the best-quality plywood) and the resulting atmosphere has what Production Designer Grant Major thinks of as a solid 'English' feeling: 'Conservative with a sense of permanence. It's got a slightly "Tudorish" feel to it; comfortable, woody, fussy: the kind of environment in which you might expect a character like Bilbo Baggins to be living.'

There were occasional practical difficulties in creating this atmosphere, as John Howe, who created the look of the sets, reflects: 'It's one thing to draw a round door, but *building* one posed all kinds of structural problems (especially regarding the hinges!) and the intersections of round halls and the round passages were a carpenter's nightmare!'

'Scale, I can tell you, was a really big issue!'
DAN HENNAH

Supervising Art Director Hennah is talking about an aspect of *The Lord of the Rings* that readers of Tolkien's book take for granted, but which, for the film-maker, was to become a major challenge: that of having characters of substantially different sizes appearing in scenes together.

Tolkien was surprisingly vague about sizes: describing a hobbit's height as varying between two and four foot but mentioning one of Pippin's ancestors who was four foot five. If the name of *The Lord of the Rings* production company, Three Foot Six, were anything to go by, you might suppose that to be the height of a hobbit, but model sheets for the films showing 'Character Comparative Heights', depict hobbits as standing at an average of four foot two inches, with Dwarves at four foot six inches and Elves at six foot two inches. Orc heights vary – according to breed – between five foot two inches and six foot six inches while a Ringwraith measures up at six foot nine inches and a cave troll at ten foot tall.

Scenes in which a hobbit was required to appear alongside a human immediately posed the question of how those differences in scale could be shown on screen. An obvious solution would have been to cast small actors as small characters as was done in films like *Legend* and *Willow*, but Peter Jackson decided at an early stage that was not a route he wanted to take. In the end, the film-makers came up with a variety of different solutions to problems of scale – some involving the latest computer technology, others as old as cinema itself.

The most traditional technique involved 'forced perspective' which enabled a hobbit-height Frodo to be seen sitting

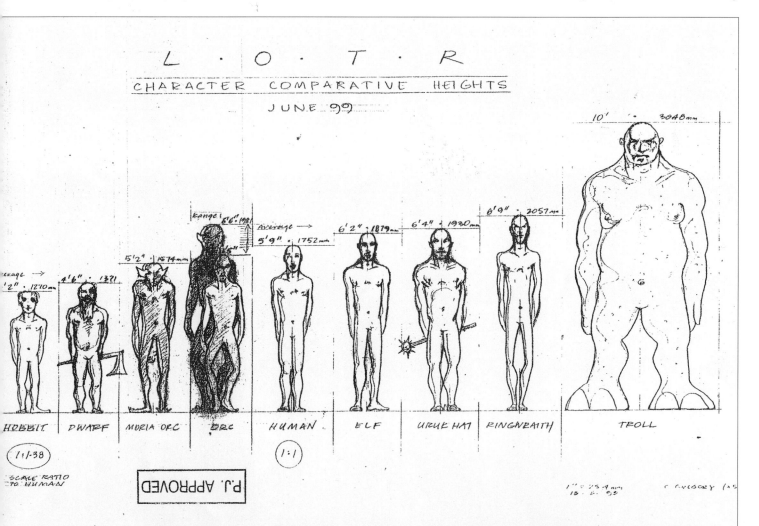

and talking to the much larger Gandalf. Forced perspective is achieved by placing Sir Ian McKellen, playing Gandalf, considerably nearer to the camera than Elijah Wood as Frodo. The eye of the camera fails to 'read' the gap of several feet between the two actors and, instead, shows them on film as if they were sitting opposite one another but with one smaller in stature to the other.

Another technique utilized in films from *Mary Poppins* to *Superman* employed what is known as a blue-screen: an actor playing one of the hobbits would be filmed in front of a blue-screen and the footage then combined with film of a setting so that the hobbit appeared to be in scale.

One has only to pause and consider just how many shots were required in *The Lord of the Rings Trilogy* to show char-

Below: *The four hobbits enter the Prancing Pony Inn*

acters of different sizes in correct proportion to one anoth-er to realize the phenomenal undertaking represented by these films if for no other reason than in getting the scale of the characters right.

So, in addition to the various types of camera trickery, the film also used 'scale-doubles', substitute players dressed iden-tically to the actors playing the hobbits, only much smaller (and for some sequences dressed like the big people, only bigger) and wearing masks to replicate the features of the actors playing the parts.

A world-wide search for four-foot-high actors resulted in a talented cast of screen-doubles: Kiran Shah, Bhoja Khannada (BK), Praphaphorn Chansantor (Fon), Indravadam J Purohit, Murugan, Martin Gray, Brett Beattie, Trevor Bau and Abigail Turner who stood in, variously, for the smaller characters in scenes in which they had to appear in a scene with Elves or men and where camera-trickery couldn't be used. There was also Paul Randall, a seven-foot-one New Zealander, who stood in for Gandalf, Aragorn, Boromir and Legolas in scenes in which the hobbit actors were the focus of the shot.

'It was more than a bit strange,' says Elijah Wood, 'seeing somebody four-foot high, walking around not only dressed like me, but wearing a mask of me! What was even stranger was that the face didn't actually move, it just had this one singular expression of mine moulded onto a piece of latex! Now that was bizarre, but cool!'

Odd though the experience may have been, the charac-ter actors are full of praise for their scale-doubles. Billy Boyd's scale-double for Pippin was Fon: 'She was incredible! She would watch a tape of me acting and then the next moment she would do precisely what I did – only smaller! And that was really weird, seeing someone who looks like you from the back doing what you were doing and wearing your face – except that when you caught it from odd angles it didn't look right, because, of course, you never think you look like what you look like!'

The use of scale-doubles also resulted in a lot of 'doubling-up' for other departments: two versions of each set, built to different scales and, as Ngila Dickson explains, a great many costumes: 'We had a costume for one of the actors who was a hobbit and who was about five foot five, a reasonably normal height. We also had a scale-double for the actor who was four foot tall. Then we would have a charac-ter like Aragorn, who's six foot high, and *his* scale-double who was seven foot something. So we had to make that costume in both those sizes. But we weren't just constantly doubling-up on all the costumes in these different ratios, we also had to scale all the patterns of the cloths that they were wearing. Before we could settle any design we had to be sure we could also recreate it a third larger or a third smaller.'

a WORKSHOP of the fantastic

'**W**e pride ourselves on a certain level of fanaticism that we bring to our work.' Richard Taylor and his partner Tania Rodger are talking about the role played by their company, Weta Workshop Ltd, in the making of Peter Jackson's *The Lord of the Rings Trilogy*.

If Taylor and Rodger are fanatical, it is probably just as well, for they are working with a director who shares that fanaticism: 'In his own quiet way,' says Taylor, 'Peter is unrelentingly driven to create the best possible product and make a film that captures the audience's imagination – which is a very good approach when you are attempting to bring such a beloved work to the screen.'

In doing that, the 65,000 square feet of space that makes up Weta Workshop became transformed into what Taylor describes as 'a whirlwind of enthusiasm'. Over 48,000 separate items were produced for the film, including 1000 suits of armour, 2000 stunt weapons and over 2,200 pairs of prosthetic hobbit-feet!

The only independent company working on the film, Weta Workshop has also been responsible for special make-up effects, for the film's miniatures and for the design, manufacture and operation of creatures and animatronics.

'At the height of production on *The Lord of the Rings*,' recalls Richard Taylor, 'we had a workshop crew of 148 with another 45 people on set. We were servicing all the units filming on the four miniature-stages as well as those at four or five different outside locations. On any one day, we were dressing up to 500 actors in Weta product, which often included over 200 people in full head-to-toe body prosthetics!'

The story of Weta Workshop Ltd began in 1985. A year of making puppets for television commercials led to an introduction to Peter Jackson, who was then preparing for his feature about an anarchic TV puppet show, *Meet the Feebles*. 'It was a crazy film!' laughs Rodger. 'It had a great story, a brilliant script and the whole crew were young and enthusiastic. It was our first film and we really relished it!'

Below: *Weta Logo, Richard Taylor and Tania Rodger; with hair, make-up and armour in place, Lurtz is ready for action*
Opposite: *Used prosthetic feet waiting for the shredder; a rack of 'deep background' Orc masks*

After *Meet the Feebles*, Taylor and Rodger worked on the (decidedly gory) special effects for Peter Jackson's next film, *Braindead*, 'which,' says Rodger, 'really allowed us to push the boundaries of our imaginations.'

The next film on which Taylor and Rodger collaborated with Jackson was *Heavenly Creatures*. The Oscar-nominated film counterpointed the true-life events surrounding a brutal murder committed by two young girls in New Zealand during

Left: The inspiration for the hobbit-holes' design: John Howe's painting of the interior of Bag End

the 1950s, with surreal images of a parallel fantasy-world inhabited by the young murderers.

By this time, the operation had considerably outgrown the original two-person outfit: 'Suddenly,' recalls Rodger, 'it wasn't just Richard and me working on these films; it required a facility – a workshop – and we began employing the kind of people who enjoyed doing the things that we enjoyed!'

Along with the development of physical effects, the workshop needed and attracted people skilled in the rapidly-developing area of computer effects technology. Both disciplines were harnessed to create a cast of ghostly characters for Peter Jackson's *The Frighteners*. It was following the making of this film that the concept emerged of the twin-faceted organization that is Weta Workshop and Weta Digital, and in this new form the workshop was well prepared for supporting Jackson when he decided he was going to film *The Lord of the Rings*. 'There was absolutely no doubt in my mind,' says Taylor, 'that Weta had to look after as many of the departments on the film as possible. I just knew that if the work was dissipated around the effect-shops of the world that we would never succeed in encapsulating Tolkien's vision.' It seemed an insane idea, but it was born out of a desire to bring to the making of these films a singular Tolkienesque brush-stroke.'

This synergy is reinforced by Weta's complementary partnership between physical and digital effects: 'The crossover between the departments,' says Taylor, 'was as simple as walking through a door into the next room. The cross-pollination of ideas throughout the facility provided the over-arching strength to our work on *The Lord of the Rings*.'

Peter Jackson agrees: 'Making a big movie like this, is rather like a military operation: the difference between success and failure often depends on communication. Hundreds of people need to share information, so lines of communication must be clear, open and direct. One of the big advantages that we have is the close proximity of all of the key components: I was able to be shooting or editing a scene for the film, and then, within a few minute's drive, be looking at props and models or viewing an effects-shot as it came off the computer. Having this infrastructure has been a key factor in making this project work.'

A special atmosphere was generated at Weta, during the filming of the trilogy: 'There were days,' says Tania Rodger, 'when the moment you came through the workshop door,

you would think: "I'm here! I've arrived in Middle-earth!"'

Summing up Weta Workshop's achievements on *The Lord of the Rings Trilogy*, Richard Taylor says: 'We have treated this entire project with a level of religious fervour. It has been a crusade and I'm adamant that we have not been making a movie, but creating a legacy!'

'Because we want to give The Lord of the Rings a historical rather than a fantasy feel,' says Producer Barrie Osborne, 'all the props are being created with great care.'

The 'Props' (or 'properties') in a film are all those things that are used by the actors in their roles or are seen as part of the set-decoration. On most movies – even some period films – these will simply be bought or hired. For *The Lord of the Rings Trilogy*, all the props were designed and hand-crafted: made to order – from scratch.

Led by Props Master Nick Weir, and Head Furniture Maker John Shearman, a hard-working team of prop-makers have been busily producing everything from rustic tables and chairs to ornate Elven candlesticks, employing the skills of a great many local artisans, including potters, glass-blowers, metal and leather-workers.

Whether a chair for a hobbit-hole or a crown for a king, all the props in *The Lord of the Rings Trilogy* required the director's personal sanction. 'Peter is interested in every single thing in the picture,' says Dan Hennah. 'There isn't a sword, a saddle, a flag or a spear that he hasn't seen and approved.'

The visual inspiration for many of those props was drawn from the paintings and designs of Alan Lee and John Howe. Also, as Richard Taylor of Weta Workshop explains, the film's Art Department referred to Tolkien's own artwork: 'Where, for example, he drew a badge of honour for the house of an Elven family, we have replicated it and incorporated it into various design elements in the film. I like to think that with such details, as well as enhancing the look of the film, we are paying homage to the incredibly creative mind of J R R Tolkien.'

THE ONE RING

'One Ring to rule them all,

One Ring to find them…'

'The Ring itself, the One Ring,' says Weta Workshop's Richard Taylor, 'is a very significant image in the film: so powerful, so fundamental to the story but such a simple ring.'

Described by Tolkien as being made of pure and solid gold, the Ring is quite plain, without any markings – except when, by the use of fire, Gandalf reveals the Elvish inscription: 'One Ring to bring them all and in the darkness bind them.'

The 'Lord of the Rings' of the title is the Dark Lord, Sauron, who forged the One Ring in the fires of Mount Doom so that he might use its great and terrible magic to find and seize control of the other rings of power that had been crafted, years earlier, by the Elven-smiths and worn – for good and ill – by Elves, Dwarves and men. Some of those rings had come into Sauron's hand, and others had eluded his grasp; but he had lost the One Ring and for many years knew nothing of its whereabouts until it passed from Gollum to Mr Bilbo Baggins…

Given the significance of the Ring, Peter Jackson and his colleagues knew that its visual representation within the films was of great importance. The task of designing the One Ring was undertaken by Grant Major and the Art Department, while the fiery letters which magically appear upon its surface were created by the technicians at Weta Digital Ltd.

'Beautiful in its simplicity,' says Richard Taylor, 'it perfectly captures how I envisaged the One Ring. The fact that, embodied within this single, tiny trinket is a power so all-encompassing that it is able to alter not just the course of history, not just the fate of these characters, but that of all Middle-earth.'

In directing sequences featuring the Ring, Jackson employed a variety of film-making tricks to give the One Ring weight and potency: 'This is just a regular-sized ring and yet you have to convey the power that makes it more than just a piece of metal on somebody's hand. So every time we show the Ring, I use a close-up, I get in very tight with the camera so that it seems much bigger. In addition, there are sound-effects with which we have created a presence, a sense that the Ring is alive and can almost be heard breathing!'

> *'The first thing I had to do was a sword fight. Even before I spoke a single word of dialogue, I was forced to confront the physicality of my character.'*
>
> VIGGO MORTENSEN

Viggo Mortensen is recalling his first day's shooting on *The Lord of the Rings Trilogy*: the sword-fight on Weathertop when Aragorn (or as he calls himself then, 'Strider') defends Frodo and the other hobbits from an attack by the evil Ringwraiths.

'It was probably helpful to do something physical before speaking,' says Mortensen. 'More than any other character, Aragorn's actions speak for him. His choices, the decisions he makes, his physicality, his body, tell you a lot about him. He's a man who throws himself into situations. Which, is why it was good to begin my work with a sword-fight.'

Richard Taylor, Director of Weta Workshop, considers the amazing array of swords and weapons that have been produced for *The Lord of the Rings Trilogy*. 'A sword is a very interesting prop, because not only does it have to look aesthetically beautiful or aesthetically crude (depending upon which army it was manufactured for) it also has to be

Above: *Peter Jackson directs Viggo Mortensen as Aragorn*
Left: *Boromir's swords stand ready for use*

a workable object, undergoing the most intense rigors on a daily basis.'

Conceptual Artist John Howe was keen that the swords used in these films should not conform to the predictable Hollywood weaponry: 'Film swords are almost always great big, ugly, blunt things that you could never move if they were actually made of metal. A sword should have balance and a grace and beauty in every line.'

Skilled swordsmith Peter Lyons created all the sprung steel blades for the swords used by Aragorn and the other warriors in the story. Employing methods of hand-grinding identical to those used by ancient swordsmiths, Lyons captured the authentic shape and an antique feel but with the vitality of a sword new-forged.

It is a vitality that can capture an actor's imagination. 'Viggo is never very far away from his sword. He treats it with tremendous respect and it's almost as if he were respecting the skills that went into its making,' says Tania Rodger, Manager of Weta Workshop. 'Remembering the day when I watched the sword being made in the workshop, I find it fascinating to see the realistic way in which Viggo uses it and how he has made it a part of his character.'

Billy Boyd (Pippin) with Sword Master Bob Anderson

'Aragorn's sword,' says Richard Taylor, 'is first and foremost a functional item, something with which to defend oneself against a foe. And Viggo totally embraced the culture surrounding the use of a sword and treats it as if his own life depends on it!'

The Sword Master on *The Lord of the Rings Trilogy* was a legendary Hollywood name: Bob Anderson, whose career includes stunt work on *From Russia with Love*, *The Empire Strikes Back* and *The Return of the Jedi*; serving as fencing coach on *Barry Lyndon* and Sword Master for such swashbuckling pictures as *Highlander*, *The Three Musketeers* and *The Mask of Zorro*.

'We waited for Bob Anderson with some trepidation,' recalls Richard Taylor. 'We knew that our product was good and were happy with it, but we hadn't yet had it tested by the best! I believe he was also a little apprehensive that this bunch of Kiwi guys whom he knew nothing about at the bottom end of the world, could have produced weaponry that would meet his exacting standards. But it is a great compliment to the technicians at Weta that, over the length of the filming, there have been so few breakages that Bob Anderson complimented us on having made some of the best swords he had ever used.'

In addition to the swords used by the central characters, more than two thousand background weapons were also produced for *The Lord of the Rings Trilogy*, mainly employed in the dramatic battle scenes which will be seen in *The Two Towers* and *The Return of the King*.

Cast in a semi-rigid urethane these particular items proved virtually indestructible, whilst not looking as if they were made of anything other than steel. 'I was adamant,' says Richard Taylor, 'that I could provide Peter Jackson with background weapons that – if he pushed the camera through the crowd till he reached the actors in the deep background – the armour and weapons would stand up to tight close-ups and not give away the fact that they were only manufactured out of rubber!'

In helping create the armour designs for *The Lord of the Rings Trilogy*, John Howe's aim was simple, if not easily achieved: 'Although the Middle-earth setting is clearly that of a fantasy, we struggled to make the armour convincing – and, hopefully, to avoid as many as possible of the all-too-familiar clichés.'

Background armour created for the Elvish army of the Second Age

Previous: *The Ringwraiths — the actors' masks will be digitally removed*
Above: *Detail of Ringwraith gauntlets*

'Because the technicians at Weta Workshop were based in New Zealand,' says Richard Taylor, 'a young country that lacks cultural roots to the history and literature of medieval Europe, they were initially relying, for their armour references, on some photographs from museums, a few books they had read and one or two films they had seen.' Then John Howe arrived…

Howe's fascination with armoury began in the late 70s when, for the first time, he saw some suits of armour in a museum: 'I couldn't believe those things! What a crazy notion to make oneself into a crustacean, in a metal shell! But what I really fell for was their beauty. There is no crude historical armour; the real thing, even the cheapest pieces, are ingeniously inventive but, at the same time, economic and functional.'

John Howe's aesthetic appreciation of armour was complemented by his practical knowledge. Unknown to anyone before his arrival in New Zealand, Howe was active in the Companie of Saynte George, a voluntary association in his Swiss homeland dedicated to recreating life within a small fifteenth century military castle garrison. Working with museums and castles throughout Europe, the Companie recreate an impression of everyday medieval life in meticu-

lous detail: from authentic armour and weapons to bedding, personal possessions and period underwear – or lack of it! No wonder Richard Taylor describes John Howe's arrival on *The Lord of the Rings* project as 'a fundamental, life-changing event for Weta Workshop's Armour Division!'

The challenge was to create functional armour that looked authentic but also different. 'At every stage,' says Taylor, 'we tried to step outside what we've seen in our own history and create armour that was not of our world. We've drawn on some of the best design-elements from armour and weapons throughout our own times whilst avoiding the trap of producing what fits people's perceptions of "classic historical armour".'

Designing armour is one thing, building it is quite another. But Weta Workshop decided to begin exactly where the process would have begun in medieval times: 'We set up a foundry,' says Taylor, 'and we employed two armour-smiths to hand-beat all the original armour out of plate steel. By using hammer, anvil and the furnace we were able to get the kind of shapes and forms, the fluting and all the detailing that would have been created in times past.'

Silicon moulds were then taken from the metal armour and, with the aid of a polyurethane spraying machine, some 48,000 separate pieces of armour were produced. Whilst Weta have used modern technology to mass-produce the vast number of items required to equip the armies of Middle-earth, the decision to begin with a smith hammering white-hot steel into shape on an anvil has added an authentic look that other fantasy film-makers will envy.

'These guys probably get less sleep than anybody, work harder and complain less than anybody on the whole production!' Viggo Mortensen is talking about the films' horse-wranglers. 'Wherever we're filming – up a mountain or out in the desert – that's where they have to take the horses. They have to get them there before we arrive, feed and water them, and, when we're all through filming, bring them back again.'

The Lord of the Rings Trilogy boasts a impressive equine cast: from Sam's solid little pony, Bill, to the fearful black steeds ridden by the Ringwraiths. There are also horses for heroes and wizards and Elves: 'When I was a kid,' says Orlando Bloom, 'I hacked around a bit: just jumped on a horse and,

with his mount: 'The first time in front of the cameras, he was not keen. But he turned out to be quite a ham, because by the second time we had to do something on film, it seemed like he was looking for the camera: he was rearing up, showing off and obviously couldn't get enough of it!'

Although Mortensen did a lot of riding as a child he never learned 'English style', using both reins: 'I'm used to neck-reining, that's riding single-handed, which is what you need to be able to do if you're using a sword or a spear: you use your other hand to control the horse, reining him in, wheeling him around. So, we were used to different techniques – the horses and I – but we taught each other and learned from each other.'

'I have the most exquisite costumes.
At one stage, I was getting a bit worried
because I was actually spending more time
in wardrobe than I was on set!'

HUGO WEAVING

'Can I think of a more difficult job than this?' asks Ngila Dickson, Costume Designer on *The Lord of the Rings Trilogy*. 'No! *Cleopatra* might have been tough, but compared to this…' An experienced designer whose previous work includes Peter Jackson's feature, *Heavenly Creatures*, and the television series *Hercules* and *Xena, Warrior Princess*, Dickson looks back to the point when she joined the project: 'The best thing I can say, is "Thank God for naiveté!" Despite working on big costume shows for quite a while, I really think if I'd known then what I know now, I would have gone away and done something else!'

The task was daunting: costuming more than twenty leading characters, dozens of supporting roles and thousands of extras for three movies, which were to be filmed, more or less, concurrently. There were also the demands imposed upon a costume designer by the fact that Tolkien's story is a journey that from the time when Frodo sets out on his quest to his final struggle on Mount Doom in the Land of Mordor

The hobbits' clothes are designed using comfortable, natural fabrics in rustic colours

"Yee-ha!" off I'd go! But I really got serious about horses while making these films. Over a two-month period, I trained on between fifteen and twenty different horses – sort of working my way up!'

It was a demanding process, but one which Bloom – who plays the Elf, Legolas – was determined to master: 'I really wanted to become a competent rider so that I could play Legolas as convincingly as possible. It was a hard process to reach a standard where I was capable of the things that Legolas would do, such as riding along, dropping the reins, firing a bow and arrow, and taking up the reins again and riding off. That is not easy, I can tell you!'

Viggo Mortensen – who, as Aragorn, plays several dramatic scenes on horseback – also spent time getting acquainted takes six months and two days. It is a journey that leads the characters across a rugged terrain: down rivers, through woods and over snowy mountain passes to marshland and parched wastes of volcanic ash.

The length of that journey and the conditions through which the characters travel, necessitated the making of several versions of each costume in order to show the wear and tear that they would have undergone.

'I can remember an early meeting about budgets,' recalls Dickson, 'when I said I was going to need a minimum of ten versions of Frodo's costume alone and everybody tried to shoot me down in flames!' During the course of a year's filming she has been proved right. Indeed, Dickson's initial estimates were exceeded, because for each version of Frodo's costume, extra copies had to be produced for Frodo's body-double, stunt-double and horse-double; while, for his scale-double, those costumes had to be produced with every last detail – from button-holes and embroidered patterning to rips and tears – recreated in a smaller scale. No wonder Dickson describes the volume of costumes that have been gone through as 'colossal'.

It may have taken Dickson a little time to realize the full extent of the job she had taken on but there was no doubt about the 'look' that she would be aiming to deliver. 'Peter wanted it to be a very real world,' Dickson recalls, 'so that audiences would believe that what they were seeing really existed like an alternative reality, or a world before this world.'

Jackson recognizes that his requirements were demanding: 'I wanted the costumes to feel more historically-based than fantasy-based. But having said that, I also didn't want it to be boringly historical, because it has to be a history we've never seen before, it's a mythic history.' Ngila Dickson, therefore, faced the difficult task of creating a wardrobe of costumes that had a historical feel without representing any recognizable period and which must never look, as Jackson puts it, like 'that cheesy fantasy we so often see in movies'.

Dickson's first challenge was the hobbits. 'How do you make a costume work when they've got big ears and big feet?' Dickson's solution was to design costumes that reflected the characters' country life-style: 'I decided to make their costumes very textural, to use natural fabrics with really strong weaves. I wanted the hobbits' clothes to be woolly and woven and quilted, to have a rustic feeling and to be colourful in a harvesty-kind of way: golden yellows and greens

The Lady Galadriel

through to a maroony-brown which became Frodo's colour.'

Finding a costume colour for Frodo helped establish his character as being a little apart from the other hobbits: Ngila Dickson's 'maroony-brown' serving like royal scarlet or imperial purple to suggest that he was like 'the young prince of the hobbits'. Dickson also had clear ideas about Frodo's companions: 'Sam is the most woolly and solidly into the earth of the hobbits, while the other two are kind of lads-about-town. Merry is the most laddish and Pippin is the most wannabe-laddish!'

All their costumes had one thing in common – they accentuated the smallness of their stature. Jacket-sleeves and trouser-legs were all just too short, waistlines and pockets were all slightly high. As Jackson puts it: 'I wanted clothes to look "lived-in", to feel that the hobbits were wearing jackets that they'd worn for fifteen years and had patched up; to have an organic reality.'

That organic feel was created partly through Dickson's choice of materials.

'Wherever possible,' notes Jackson, 'Ngila has used the types of fabrics that the various people would have actually been able to make themselves. She hasn't, for example, dressed the hobbits in any materials that, within their culture, they would be unable to produce. At the same time, she's used some wonderful fabrics to create a look for the Elves that reflects their ethereal nature and their ability to create things of great beauty.'

'In many ways,' says Dickson, 'the Elves are the angels of the story, so we were constantly searching for that ethereal quality, looking for that aura. The Elves are tall and elegant and they have a certain androgynous look: whilst it's quite clear that they are male and female, there is a sense in which their sexuality remains a kind of floating image. So, we've dressed them in layers of fine, delicate fabrics, in colours that are light and semi-shimmery and that evoke their environment.'

No character better epitomizes the Elven-nature than the Lady Galadriel, played in the film by Cate Blanchett. 'For me,' says Ngila Dickson, 'she was to be all about light. She's an older woman – how many thousand years has Galadriel been around? – and yet she is an extraordinarily young, beautiful presence. So I have given Galadriel very, very beaded frocks, they are always on incredibly light fabrics, so as not to lose that translucency to her character.'

Sometimes the contrasting costume styles help define the distinctions between the different races of Middle-earth. 'I see Legolas the Elf and Gimli the Dwarf as my opposing forces: I've got tall and slender and I've got short and squat; I've got incredibly light and I've got sunk into the earth! That, for me, is the difference between Elf and Dwarf. So, what we did with Gimli was bring him further and further

Top: *Ngila Dickson created costumes for the Dwarves in dark, earthy colours*
Above: *The Elves wear robes in sylvan shades: mossy greens and birch-bark grey*

to the earth, creating a square, a block; whereas with Legolas all our thinking was to do with his being light and fleet.'

Those stylistic concepts were then carried through to the types and colours of material chosen for the characters' costumes: 'When you look at Gimli,' says Dickson, 'you have chunky leather, darker colours, solidity; when you look at Legolas, you have lightness, pale mossy greens and greys and a slightly silvery fabric.'

Probably the most demanding costume assignment was that designed for Gandalf. 'There are so many drawings of Gandalf,' reflects Ngila Dickson, 'that I didn't know what I could bring to the character. Eventually I decided that I might take one of those images that are so familiar to people and, rather than trying to precisely recreate it, I could simply try to bring that image alive.'

That image was a painting by Conceptual Artist John Howe. Made several years before the film was even a possibility, the picture shows Gandalf striding along through a rainy Middle-earth landscape: flowing robes and billowing cloak; a tall, conical, broad-brimmed hat; wind-blown hair and a big bushy beard that falls to below the waist.

That image came, in turn, from Tolkien's own description of the wizard. Whilst being the most sensible place to begin designing the character, it also raised a few questions as Sir Ian McKellen who plays Gandalf, explains: 'Tolkien describes "a tall pointed blue hat, a long grey cloak, and a silver scarf. He had a long white beard…" But how tall is "tall"? How long is "long"? And how practical in a high New Zealand wind, are "bushy eyebrows that stuck out beyond the brim of his hat"?'

Repeated scrutiny of John Howe's Gandalf painting also gave Ngila Dickson pause: 'Part of me thought, "This is a really silly thing to do!" Because that hat is the most extreme hat of all the various depictions of Gandalf! Luckily we have a wonderful milliner here who took that task and produced a hat that helped create a fabulous image.'

Dickson was, nevertheless, well aware that, for Ian McKellen, the hat would be a challenge: 'When we first presented him with the hat, I really think he just didn't know what on earth to make of it, or how he could make it work. To have to perform from under the brim of an enormous hat is asking more than is fair of any actor. But Peter Jackson

really grew to love that hat, so the hat is there a lot more than we thought it was going to be! And Sir Ian, who knew that the hat was a huge part of the character, has lived and worked with it and, somehow, beaten it into shape – although I suspect it's been something of a love-hate relationship!'

Gandalf's costume, together with his make-up, went through various transmogrifications. Only when it had been finalized and McKellen was wearing it, did the actor notice that something was missing. It was that silver scarf that

John Howe's Gandalf from the UK paperback cover of The Lord of the Rings

Tolkien had mentioned. 'Somehow,' he recalls, 'it had been overlooked or decided against. Until I looked the part, I hadn't missed it either. And there's a thing to ponder: what does a man with an umbrella of a hat and a warm cloak need with a scarf? The story starts in autumn. We were filming in summertime. But weather conditions aside, I thought he might have the silver scarf much as he has the pointy hat – to disguise himself. The Gandalf who visits his old friends Bilbo and Frodo has lots of props. Already I have had to cope

Howe's Gandalf, played by Sir Ian McKellen, recreated by Peter Jackson

with his staff, his toffees (a non-Tolkien addition) and his pipe, so why not a scarf to do some magic with?'

The relationship between an actor and his or her costume is always personal and particular: 'There's an incredible moment,' says Ngila Dickson, 'when you see an actor settle into the character and begin to grow into their costume.' For Ian McKellen it was finding the scarf and taking on that troublesome hat; for Viggo Mortensen, playing Aragorn, it was the decision to wear his costume when he went riding during his time off set, indeed to live in it as much as possible, so that it became not something he put

on to become his character, but something that was as much a part of his character as his own skin – although few actors ever offer, as Mortensen did, to look after their own costume and keep it washed and repaired!

Ngila Dickson who first read *The Lord of the Rings* many years earlier, admits that when she first heard of the film project, she had her doubts: 'Part of me said, "Oh, my God! How can you possibly do it? Well I think Peter Jackson's done it. And to be a part of that process is phenomenal.'

# of wizard-beards and elf-ears

'I just knew that playing Gimli was going to mean four or five hours in make-up.' John Rhys-Davies is reflecting on the major drawback to playing a Dwarf in *The Lord of the Rings Trilogy*. 'The agents said "No! They are going to get it down to about an hour!" But, of course, if you believe agents, you'll believe anything! So, there we are: fantastic part, wonderful character; but a real killer in terms of make-up.'

Arriving on set each day at 4.00 am and spending the next six hours in make-up gives Rhys-Davies a head-start on all his co-stars. However, the transformation, once complete, is extraordinary and a tribute to the work of the prosthetic make-up artists at Weta Workshop, who also provided noses for Gandalf and Saruman, monstrous orc features, hobbit feet and Elf-ears.

Other make-up and hair requirements were designed by Peter Owen and Peter King. Between them, Owen and King have created make-up for theatre, opera, television and cinema, with film-credits that include *The Draughtsman's Contract*, *Dangerous Liaisons*, *The Bird Cage*, *Little Voice*, *Velvet Goldmine* and *Sleepy Hollow*, and their experience in creating hair and make-up for productions with a historical setting has been a considerable asset to the film trilogy.

'Costume and make-up,' observes Sir Ian McKellen, 'are a great aid to feeling right. It's quite familiar to me now: looking in the mirror and seeing Gandalf and not myself. It's like changing your voice, or your walk, or the way you think.'

At the outset of the project, however, a great deal of thought and discussion was devoted to devising a make-up for Gandalf. McKellen, sitting in the make-up chair, preparing for a screen-test had a disquieting experience: 'Alien visages stared back at me from the mirror – hirsute off-beats like Shylock, Fagin and Ben Gunn. Even Rasputin for a moment.'

John Rhys-Davies as Gimli

The initial results were not satisfactory: 'The beard,' he says, 'was clearly too long and cumbersome for Gandalf, the man of action – he is forever tramping and riding and on the move. I didn't want a beard which hampered me by taking on a life of its own every time the winds blew.'

For a second screen-test, Peter Owen 'care-freely slashed' the beard and cut back on the whiskers that were hiding Gandalf's cheeks. 'Once he had trimmed it all back,' Sir Ian recalls, 'I saw a glimmer of the old wizard's sternness. I smiled and tried a Gandalf twinkle, as the friend of the hobbits who admires their spirit and sociability.'

The make-up designed for *The Lord of the Rings Trilogy* was about helping to create illusions and work transformations: turning Orlando Bloom, a young actor with a black Mohican hair-cut, into the golden-haired Legolas; giving Hugo Weaving a pair of elegant ear-tips for his portrayal of the Elf-lord, Elrond; transforming Kiwi extras into orcs and uruk-hai; or taking a group of lads from England and America and making them into hobbits from the Shire: 'The first day I got to wear the wig, the fake ears and the fake feet,' recalls Elijah Wood, playing Frodo, 'it was like: "This is so cool! I've got prosthetic feet."'

stand in puddles for too long, then your feet get *really* cold!'

Whatever the drawbacks to the hobbit make-up, the actors are all agreed about the end result. 'Once you're in all of the gear,' says Sean Astin, 'once your ears are bigger and particularly once your feet are bigger – because you have to

The process of transition, however, was scarcely a speedy one: 'Getting into your feet,' says Billy Boyd, playing Pippin, 'took over an hour every morning of every day. It would be 4.30 a.m. and you'd have to stand still with your own feet inside a pair of rubber feet! That was strange! Still, at least I got through a lot of books!'

According to Dominic Monaghan, who plays Merry, the prosthetic feet, once on, were surprisingly easy to get used to: 'Just slightly bigger than our normal feet, they are hairy and relatively malleable, so you can walk – even run – in them. There's a thick layer of latex rubber underneath which protects your feet and keeps the wet out. Mind you, if you

Left: *Sir Ian McKellen as Gandalf*
Above: *Hobbit feet*

walk differently – it's quite easy to make the mental leap from being a human to being a hobbit.'

'That's why it's worth it,' agrees Elijah Wood, 'because, when it's all done, we look like hobbits – and feel like hobbits!' Then, recalling a particular experience while filming on location, he adds: 'I had a bit of a break and took a stroll to my trailer. I was walking alone in this beautiful field and I just looked down at my feet and stopped. It was the first time that I felt like a hobbit. It was bizarre, but – just for moment – I imagined that I really was a hobbit.

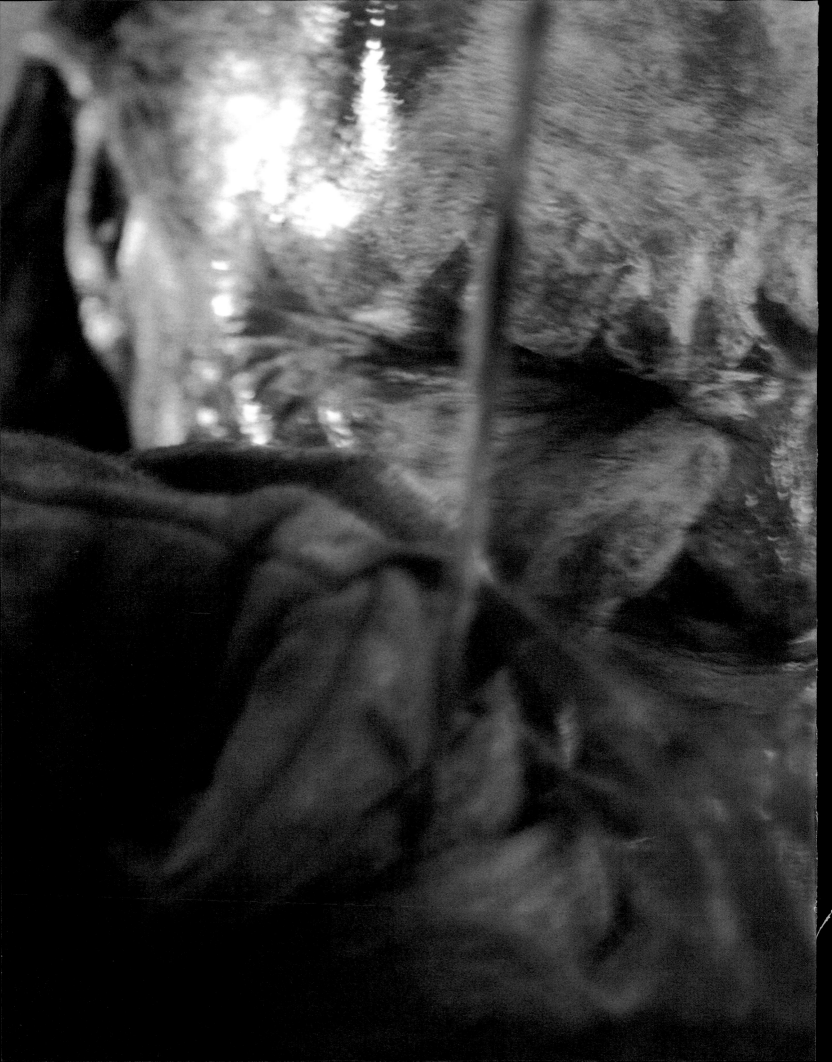

speaking the languages
of middle-earth

for many readers, part of the fascination of *The Lord of the Rings* is the thoroughness with which Tolkien created his fictional world: making maps, setting out genealogies and, most complex of all, devising the various alphabets and languages used by the different races in the story.

In addition to Westron, the Common Speech of Middle-earth (or English), there are two forms of Elvish – known as Quenya and Sindarin – the language of the Dwarves and the 'Black Speech' of Sauron's Mordor, all of which are encountered in the trilogy. This presented a daunting challenge to Dialogue and Creative Language Coaches Andrew Jack and Roísín Carty.

'Elvish is not a language we commonly deal with!' explains Jack. 'We usually teach people accents, and if we have to teach a language then it's always something we're already aware of, such as French, Italian, or German.'

Luckily for Jack and Carty, the final volume of *The Lord of the Rings* contains extensive appendices in which Tolkien gave explicit instructions on the writing and speaking of the languages used by the characters in his book. In addition, there are a number of recordings of Tolkien himself reading extracts from the book: 'It was all there in the appendices,' says Jack, 'all the stress patterns, the pronunciation and how that changes if a word has more than one consonant. Everything was there – all the information – almost as if it were inviting us to make a movie!'

Orlando Bloom, playing Legolas, enjoyed the challenge of learning and speaking Elvish: 'It was a lot of fun trying to learn it, but it wasn't easy – you have to think about phonetics, and where the stresses fall. But when you get the flow of it, it sounds beautiful.'

In playing Aragorn – a man who was raised by Elves – it was necessary for Viggo Mortensen to learn to speak Elvish fluently. Luckily, having something of a gift for languages (Mortensen is tri-lingual in English, Danish and Spanish), he found himself perfectly at ease with the language: 'It's a musical language, harmonious, mellifluous. I asked to speak more of it whenever possible, especially since there are so many scenes in the first movie featuring Elves. It's good to use the language because it's something that's not been used in film before and, if it's done well, it will involve the audience and help convey the sense of a different world.'

One of the difficulties with finding voices for the characters is that readers of the book tend to have their own clear ideas about how the characters should sound. For the hobbits it was decided to find an English rural accent. 'We decided to go for West Country,' recalls Jack, 'and we plumped for Gloucestershire

because it's not difficult to speak and it's easy to understand.'

The primary aim in establishing the accents used in the film was, as Andrew Jack explains, to convey a sense of the story unfolding in a world and an era that is different from our own: 'We have striven to create a vocal sound that is timeless and free of the influences of modern speech, so that when people go into the cinema and enter that world, they will not be reminded of their own.'

The cast worked hard at often boringly repetitive work involving word-lists and exercises, labours which were carried over into their free time when the Americans in particular were encouraged to order dinner in an English accent! 'Getting the actors to use the accents in their spontaneous speech,' says Carty, 'meant that they were able to cope with anything on set and weren't tied to only doing the accent with the written dialogue.'

As well as consulting Tolkien's written sources, Jack and Carty had access to a number of Tolkien language specialists who provided vocal pronunciation guides to help the actors speak the various character and place names according to the author's preferences.

Lists of correct pronunciations were drawn up but, as Jack points out, it was not easy to get the vast number of people working on the film to learn – and *remember* – how to say all the names correctly: 'Whenever anyone – the director, the producers, the technicians – mentioned a name, they would do it in their own, unique way which was usually not how the actor had now been told to do it! We had an awful lot of "Gandolfs" and no end of people saying, "Le-*go*lass"! So someone would (correctly) ask: "Should Legolas be standing here?" and back would come the answer: "No, Le-*go*lass should be over there." We were fighting a battle the entire time!'

cameras in middle-earth

'He's an amazing guy!

He's cool as an elf, he's got the heart of a hobbit and he's mad like a wizard!'

ORLANDO BLOOM

Video Documentarian Costa Botes, who has been filming Jackson at work on the film trilogy is well-placed to assess the man's skills: 'There are those who under-estimate Peter Jackson because he may appear shaggy and unkempt; but you don't need to watch him for very long to see that there's an incredible cinematic intelligence and creativity at work.'

'He's 100% obsessed,' says Supervising Art Director Dan Hennah. 'He gives total attention to every detail and holds a picture of every scene in his head.'

The adjectives applied to the director of *The Lord of the Rings Trilogy* are diverse and even, occasionally, contradictory: Elijah Wood talks of Jackson's 'excitement' and 'energy', whilst describing him as 'relaxed' and 'laid back'; some actors like the fact that he allows them to find and develop their own charac-ter, others appreciate the way he suggests different approaches to playing a part.

To all his players Jackson seems to convey confidence and exude a sense of security, even when making demands of them: 'He's incredibly exacting,' says Cate Blanchett, 'and a perfectionist, which I admire and warm to; but he's also very good humoured. If you look at his filmography you see the work of a man with a wicked sense of humour and a taste for the bizarre and the absurd that's absolutely vital for any director who is tackling these stories.'

'He's a bundle of fun,' says Sir Ian McKellen. 'I know few people who enjoy laughing as much as Peter. Humour is a great part of his previous work and I think

and never losing his head, or – as Sir Ian McKellen notes – his *temper*: 'I haven't seen him edge even close to it, even though he has hundreds of people making demands on him and depending on his energy levels, which simply never seem to drop.'

As Producer Barrie Osborne observes, Jackson's New Zealander stamina seems inexhaustible: 'You'll see Peter jump out of a helicopter into knee-deep snow in shorts and bare feet or go charging up a mountain without huffing and puffing! He's in remarkable shape for someone

a good part of this as well, plus he has huge humanity and common sense and an ability to work literally most hours in the day at a level of concentration which is admirable and baffling to me.'

'What I like about him,' says Christopher Lee, 'is not only his sense of humour, but his instinct. He may suggest trying a line slightly differently, or changing the odd word, or looking there instead of here. But once you are going in the right direction, you know that the best is going to be, because his intuition is so remarkable that when he says "Excellent! Print it!" then that's it!'

Associate Producer Rick Porras, likens Jackson to a juggler, keeping umpteen balls in the air at any given time

who looks like a hobbit!'

There is no doubting that Jackson leads from the front, a quality that Ian McKellen relishes: 'I'm full of admiration for him as a workman but also as a leader and as an inspiration.'

John Rhys-Davies concurs: 'Peter has the good fortune to be one of those guys that crews and casts love working with: they actually like him, they respect him. The business of being a good director is like trying to co-ordinate a moon-landing while, at the same time being the astronaut who's travelling in the spaceship! If these films are successful, Peter is going to be acknowledged as one of the two or three finest directors in the world.'

from the director's chair

'Tolkien's The Lord of the Rings *is one story and it's three books;
the film of* The Lord of the Rings *is three movies, but one story.'*

Peter Jackson is talking about the complex task of filming three pictures at the same time. 'There have been weeks when, in a very short space of time, we were shooting scenes from Part One, Part Two and Part Three. Whilst filming a very early scene in the first picture, I might have had somebody asking me to approve a costume design for a character whom you won't see until the second film or to look at the layouts for a set in the third movie. So, I'm always simultaneously juggling the three movies.'

In addition, Jackson used satellite hook-ups to keep track of the work of up to four other film units that were shooting scenes – from any of the three pictures – often on locations several miles from where Jackson himself was filming. 'While directing on one set – usually with the actors and dialogue – the second unit might be in the middle of filming a battle scene.' Under cover of a mini-marquee, Jackson would view a small bank of monitors relaying live satellite pictures from the other film units. 'If I want to give notes about something, I just pick up the phone, talk to the unit director about what I'm seeing on screen and then go back to the scene that I am directing!'

The Lord of the Rings Trilogy is not the first multi-picture film franchise in the history of cinema – think of *Star Wars* or the Indiana Jones movies – but it is the first to be filmed at one time: 'Traditionally', says Jackson 'there has been an original movie and then sequels, usually featuring some of the same characters but a completely different story. What we're doing, in telling one story over the space of three films, is unique in that they must have a continuity, they mustn't feel like different movies – as if you were watching a completely new adventure – because you're not; you will be watching one, huge, epic story that spans almost seven hours of film.'

After many months of filming, Jackson has become used to thinking about several dozen things at once. 'It's become a way of life for me,' he says. 'But doing three movies with all the complexity and detail that is contained in these films, and having all that crunched together at the same time, is something that I'll probably never want to do again in my life! This is the first and only time!'

Not that there haven't been compensations: 'One of the great perks about being involved in a film like this – especially loving *The Lord of the Rings*, as I do – is that I actually get to walk into the House of Elrond at Rivendell. You may not spot me in the movie, but I am there – on set! I look around and see Viggo in costume as Aragorn, Elijah dressed as Frodo, Orlando as Legolas and John Rhys-Davies as Gimli. There I am, standing in Rivendell, amongst these extraordinary characters who are coming to life from the books, exactly as they should come to life! That is an amazing experience!'

*Opposite: Peter Jackson
on the throne of
Saruman the White at
Orthanc Tower*

*Below: Jackson and
scriptwriter Philippa
Boyens on set*

before the cameras rolled

The Lord of the Rings Trilogy began with a 'storyboard', an aid to film-making borrowed from the animation industry. In the earliest days of the movies, animators made rough drawings with which to plot and time their pictures. As those films grew longer and more elaborate, the number of drawings increased, until there were hundreds of sketches lying around on studio floors, propped up on desks and chairs or pinned to the walls. It was one of Walt Disney's animators, in the 1930s, who came up with the idea of pinning the story drawings onto a board. The 'storyboard' proved a great innovation: it was now easier to 'read' the story of the film and to make editorial changes – moving sequence, changing shots, altering angles, deleting individual sketches and re-drawing others.

Eventually, live-action film-makers began adopting the storyboard, initially in order to work out the logistics of complex scenes, such as the burning of Atlanta in *Gone with the Wind*. Some directors, Alfred Hitchcock among them, used storyboards to plot whole films and, today, every epic and action movie will start as a series of detailed drawings on a storyboard. Peter Jackson had full storyboards drawn up for all three films of *The Lord of the Rings Trilogy*, and then, before shooting a single frame of *The Fellowship of the Ring*, he made the entire picture as an 'animatic', which is essentially a filmed version of all the still pictures on the storyboard. One or two sequences were added in primitive computer animation, a reading of the script was recorded, borrowed music and make-shift sound-effects were added, and the finished 'film' was screened. 'The animatic,' says Jackson, 'is a wonderful tool and a real help in planning the shooting of the actual movie: you immediately get an idea whether the structure and pacing is right and whether the characters are working.'

At the same time, Weta Workshop was gearing itself into action, the films' impressive cast began to be assembled and the actors started preparing for their roles.

'We came to New Zealand,' recalls Elijah Wood, 'about six weeks prior to filming. We had daily exercises with a personal trainer, learnt how to paddle canoes and fight with swords. There were sessions on accents with the voice-coach, a lot of meetings where we talked about our characters and the script and became comfortable with the people we were playing. But what was important, was that we all experienced these things alongside one another, which brought us close together and prepared us for the relationships that we would be portraying in the film.'

Preparation for Orlando Bloom began with movement: 'That was my way into the character of Legolas. It started with my just walking around a room, finding a walk, a focus, a posture. How *does* Legolas walk? Or run? How does he sit or stand? I wanted to find a way of moving that combined elements of martial arts with something almost balletic. Legolas, as I eventually discovered him, is very quiet; he never says anything unless he has to, but he's always there: alert, poised, ready for action, capable of picking up any weapon and using it with the greatest of ease.'

For other actors it was back to the book; or, in Sir Ian McKellen's case, coming to it for the first time: 'I hadn't previously read *The Lord of the Rings*, and when I *did*, then I was looking at it as source material for the film, so it wasn't really "reading". I wasn't sitting down by the fire and getting lost in the world; I was underlining passages, making notes, thinking "What does this or that mean for Gandalf's character?" That is how I prepared for the part, and when we were filming I was constantly referring back to the book. It became my Bible and I would have it with me at all times.'

Another first-time reader of Tolkien's epic, Viggo Mortensen, also made extensive annotations. 'It's such a big book to plough through,' he says. 'I needed to make notes in order to keep track of things, to be able to compare the script and the book and make sense of what we were doing. Although there was no way in which we could put everything that is in the books, onto the screen, I knew that there were things in the text that were said by, or about, my character that would be valuable to keep in mind – whether or not they were ever in the script.'

Finally, all the preparations that *could* be made, *had* been made and – although many challenges were still to be met and many hurdles had yet to be overcome – on October 11 1999 – the first take of the first shots of *The Lord of the Rings Trilogy* was committed to film…

the ReaL feLLowship of the RING

'Everybody is just so totally engrossed in the project, dedicated to doing great work,

so proud of what they're achieving,'

SEAN BEAN

W orking alongside one another for over a year of filming, the actors playing the characters in *The Fellowship of the Ring* – the hobbits Frodo, Sam, Merry and Pippin; the men, Aragorn and Boromir; Legolas the Elf, Gimli the Dwarf and the wizard, Gandalf – have formed their own unique fellowship.

'Within the first couple of days,' recalls Elijah Wood, 'the four hobbits had bonded. I think we all knew that these relationships would get us through the experience of working together for such a long time. And we couldn't have been luckier, because we all clicked immediately and I think it really shows on the screen.'

Sean Astin, who plays Sam, agrees: 'The hobbits formed a core-relationship. We ate together, we went to pubs together and we really hung out and did crazy things together. So we became friends, a loyal and earnest brotherhood; the four of us: Elijah, Dominic, Billy and myself – oh, yes, and Orlando, because we've got an Elf in the mix too!'

Previous: *Weta Workshop's model of Elrond's House at Rivendell*

Orlando Bloom, playing Legolas, echoes Astin's sentiments: 'I'm so lucky to be working with a bunch of people you can just hang out with, inside and outside the work environment. When we're not filming together we're off surfing together, or snow-boarding, or jumping out of planes or throwing ourselves off bridges! There's a real bond of love.'

Viggo Mortensen, playing Aragorn, views the group as a family: 'Of course, family life has its ups and downs and there are times when members of the family misbehave or you have differences of opinion with them! But generally, you're all trying to get through things together and that's how you grow closer.'

The camaraderie involves quite a lot of good-natured ribbing, particularly between Aragorn and Legolas. 'We have these digs at each other,' explains Orlando Bloom with a laugh 'Viggo will go on about Elves and how they're always doing their nails and brushing their long, blond hair, and being all prissy. And I just say: "Well, at least I'm going to live forever! Got that? *Live Forever!*"'

A very particular bond developed between two other members of the Fellowship that has clearly affected their performances in the film. The fate of Frodo and Sam, as portrayed by Elijah Wood and Sean Astin, represents the emotional core of Tolkien's story. 'Our journey in making these films,' says Wood, 'mirrors the journey of Frodo and Sam. Every day we get up, come into work, put our hobbit-feet on and off we go together, side by side, every step of the way.'

Sir Ian McKellen, viewing the Fellowship with the gentle wisdom of the wizard Gandalf, acknowledges the strength of the bond that exists between them all: 'The four hobbits became instant pals and the rest of us – Legolas, Gimli, Aragorn, Boromir and myself – have been there, alongside them, the whole time and, bless them, they are all absolutely delightful in their separate ways! So there really has been a sense of fellowship and there's even talk of us all having a "Fellowship of the Ring" tattoo and, I must say, that would be one way of commemorating our friendships…'

Tattooed or not, for the actors the memory of their relationships will remain with them forever: 'We all came here,' says Elijah Wood, 'halfway around the world, in order to work on this project for over a year. It has been an amazing experience and, through it, I've made some of the best friends I'm ever likely to make in my entire life.'

'I've worked in films using a lot of special effects; but nothing like this – absolutely nothing – has ever been done before!'

Christopher Lee, playing the wizard, Saruman, is talking about the staggering use of effects in *The Lord of the Rings Trilogy*.

The films make use of just about every trick in the film-makers' book of screen-magic: this, as Richard Taylor of Weta Workshop explains, is vitally important: 'You have to keep changing the way you do things; if you don't, the audience will soon work out how they are being done!'

Many of the special effects techniques are ones that are tried and tested, although always enhanced to state-of-the-art standards that are only achievable by the use of sophisticated modern technology, much of it pushed to new frontiers in the making of these films.

For over a hundred years, film-makers have employed forced-perspective to help create illusions of scale but never so convincingly as now. Similarly, special effects techniques involving blue-screens, matte paintings and composites have been used in movies for several decades in order to give the appearance of characters being in exotic, expensive or outlandish settings or to add-in scenic and architectural details that did not exist on any set or location. Once again, however, *The Lord of the Rings Trilogy* has taken such effects to a new level of competence as well as making them virtually impossible to spot.

Many classic movies – such as *Frankenstein*, *The Wizard of Oz* and *Citizen Kane* – represented some of their locations with shots of scale models, but few films will ever equal the models made for *The Fellowship of the Ring* and its sequels. The scale miniatures created at Weta Workshop ranged in size from one or two centimetres to several meters (the latter known affectionately as 'bigatures'), and were shot on film-stages located in a vast 24,000 square foot warehouse.

An astonishing degree of detail was incorporated into the models representing such important locations in the story as Elrond's house at Rivendell, Saruman's stronghold at Isengard and the wind-swept ruins on Weathertop where Strider and the hobbits are attacked by the Black Riders.

Above: *Weathertop: the finished set*

Guided by the Director of Photography, Alex Funke, the twenty-strong Miniature Production Unit would light the model (so as to match the environment in any live-action footage) and filming would begin using special cranes and camera-rigs that enabled the technicians to create sweeping shots, moving swiftly and smoothly around the model.

In several of Peter Jackson's earlier films characters were created with puppetry, character suits and a system known as animatronics, in which models are electronically manipulated. In *The Lord of the Rings Trilogy*, however, the majority of the 'creatures' encountered by Frodo and his friends were birthed with the aid of an astonishing range of state-of the-

art computer software utilized at Weta Workshop's sister-studio, Weta Digital Ltd.

'When we're dealing with creatures,' says Tania Rodger, Manager of the Weta Workshop facilities, 'the overlap between Weta Workshop and Weta Digital involves many layers. At a time when there was less sophistication with digital effects, we would build creatures as animatronics figures that would "perform" (with the help of operators) in front of the camera. These days, with the sophistication of digital effects, the creatures we create are made into scale models, or *maquettes*, that can then be scanned into a computer and animated.'

The monsters of Middle-earth – such as the cave-troll and the Balrog which the Fellowship confront in the Mines of

Moria – were built, developed and enhanced (endowed with muscle systems and layers of textured skin) by artist-technicians sitting in front of a computer-screen. 'The digital effects,' says Rodger, 'are quite remarkable and whilst, hopefully, doing justice to the creatures as we visualized them they will also have a real sense of "life".'

Over two hundred people have contributed to the creation of the films' digital effects, and – long after the live-action filming had wrapped and the actors had gone home – they were still at work making last-minute refinements to *The Fellowship of the Ring* and creating effects for *The Two Towers* and *The Return of the King*.

Individuals experienced in art, music and technology travelled from colleges and other workshops in Europe, North America and Asia to join a core of more than 140 New Zealanders. Wherever they came from and whatever their background, they have been united by a passion for their work, and by a determination that Peter Jackson's vision for the movies should not be blocked by anything so mundane as a technical obstacle. If the desired effects could not be created by existing software programmes then, rather than divert from their ideal course, they would set about developing the hardware and software required to deliver the necessary results and, in the process, push forward the frontiers of their craft.

Four years of development and problem-solving preceded the filming and resulted in the many extraordinary effects seen in the film trilogy such as the 100,000 warriors serving with the orc armies (seen in the second and third movies) which have been brought to life with a computer programme using a 'behavioural simulation system'. Also making occasional appearances in the films, but going unnoticed, are digital versions of the members of the Fellowship. This was achieved by putting the 'real actors' into 'motion-capture suits' which enabled their various movements to be digitally recorded. Computer-generated likenesses could then be created and made to 'act' without any further assistance from their flesh and blood counterparts.

One major character who will certainly exist *only* in computerized form is perhaps Tolkien's most famous creation, Gollum. First introduced in *The Hobbit*, it was Gollum who possessed – and was possessed by – the One Ring before it came to Bilbo Baggins. As Tolkien went on to reveal in *The Lord of the Rings*, Gollum's fate was eventually bound up with that of Frodo and the Ring itself.

'Ah, yes! Gollum,' sighs Richard Taylor. 'People say: "Gollum? That's not difficult! Gollum's *easy*! Everyone knows what Gollum looks like!" Right! And there's your problem: everyone thinks they know what Gollum looks like, but everyone has different, personal idea about the character. Although lots of artists have depicted him, no one has succeeded in perfectly capturing Gollum – and yet, *that* is what we have to do!'

Audiences won't see how Weta Digital have 'captured' Gollum until the release of *The Two Towers*, meanwhile, there are plenty of strange and scary beings to be savoured in *The Fellowship of the Ring*.

Peter Jackson had very determined ideas about how all the creatures in the film trilogy should look – or *not* look: 'I really didn't want the creatures to look like "computery" monsters, when, with just a little imagination and attention to detail they could look real. In creating the cave-troll, for example, we've given him fingernails that are dirty and broken and a skin that is covered in bumps and warts and has grime in all the cracks and crevices.'

For Orlando Bloom, playing Legolas, the task of grappling with a computer-generated cave-troll in the Mines of Moria was a fun, if demanding, experience: 'I am asked to imagine this enormous creature coming at me, wielding a great mace and with a huge chain tied round his wrist that he's using like a whip! There are explosions and I'm being blown from side to side; then the chain gets caught around a column and I leap light-footedly up the chain and skip over the top of the non-existent troll's head firing arrows as I go! But basically I'm fighting something that's not really there!'

Although Peter Jackson and the teams of craftspeople and technicians at Weta Workshop and Digital have been committed to producing the most staggering effects possible, they have also been at pains to ensure that, whilst those effects are used to enhance the drama and add colour and dimension, they never become an end in themselves: 'There are a lot of special effects in these movies,' says actor Viggo Mortensen, 'but the focus has always remained on character and emotion. Essentially, this is a story about a group of individuals – men, Elves, Dwarves and hobbits – how they relate to one another and how they feel about things, what they hope for and what they fear.'

THE ROAD GOES EVER ON

'There is a parallel between the journey which the characters make in Tolkien's book and our journey as film-makers.' Filming on *The Lord of the Rings Trilogy* is almost at an end and Peter Jackson is reflecting on the four years he has been treading the road to Middle-earth. *'The epic quest which these characters embark on takes them to the point of exhaustion and collapse and, as we near the end of our journey, I think, in some respects, we're feeling the same way!'*

J R R Tolkien invested great significance in the image of the journey. It is central to many of his works, and although Tolkien discouraged attempts at read meanings into his books, it is impossible not to see parallels between 'the road of life' and the road through Middle-earth that, in *The Hobbit*, carries Bilbo off to far-flung places and dangerous adventures and which, in *The Lord of the Rings*, bears Frodo away on a perilous quest to destroy the One Ring.

Richard Taylor of Weta Workshop also sees the journey taken by the Fellowship as an analogy for that made by the cast and crew of the movie trilogy: 'Making this film has been a journey for its creators. A huge proportion of all our creative careers will have been spent working on *The Lord of the Rings*. There have been the emotional highs and lows that you get from any large group of people working on a project; the hurdles that every movie goes through; the many long hours that have gone into the making of these films and the sheer day-to-day physical exhaustion of it all. There are the houses that have been bought, the people that have got married, the children that have been born, the families that have grown: the beautiful tapestry of life that is the backdrop to the making of *The Lord of the Rings*.'

Taylor's partner, Tania Rodger, adds: 'There is not only a lot of journeying in *The Lord of the Rings*, there are discoveries that are made and there are opportunities that are seized or missed. That is a reflection on the way in which we all interpret our own journey through life. Every day offers different challenges and different opportunities and these films have offered us, as individuals, an enormous number of challenges to resolve and opportunities to further ourselves and our talents.'

Elijah Wood, after a year of playing Frodo, sees the film – like a road taken on a journey – as something to be run: 'It's like a marathon. You train for it, you jump into it and there's no stopping, no turning back. You're running, running until you get to

Opposite: *Balin's tomb in Moria*

the finish line. It may be that you will never do anything like it again, but you will always value the fact that you did it.'

And how will others – the movie-going public, the critics, the fans of *The Lord of the Rings* – view the results of this movie-making journey through Middle-earth? Conceptual Artist Alan Lee, who has been interpreting Tolkien's story for many years, has no doubts: 'People are going to come away from these films having had not just this wonderful and extraordinary adventure, but also, at the same time, a very powerful, heartfelt experience.'

Sir Ian McKellen – possibly demonstrating a wizardly foresight – also believes that the film trilogy is set for success: 'I think the quality, the depth and the complexities of Tolkien's

story which come through from the script onto the screen will mark *The Lord of the Rings* as being the daddy of all epic films – not because it's the longest, but simply because it's the best!'

It will be two years, however, before audiences around the world will be able to fully and finally appraise the film for its cumulative qualities. When *The Lord of the Rings* was first published, readers had to wait several months to see how the story that had been begun in *The Fellowship of the Ring* was continued in *The Two Towers* and then the best part of a year to know how it ended in *The Return of the King*. Ask any of those early readers why they waited patiently (and *impatiently!*) with the subsequent volumes on order at their bookshops or reserved at their libraries, and they will say it

was because the story gripped them and they couldn't bear not to know how the quest would be resolved.

The film-makers are hoping that the movie trilogy will generate a similar response: 'As the story goes along,' says Viggo Mortensen, 'it keeps growing and developing. Things escalate; each conflict and every battle has more to it. And, hopefully, by the time you come to the end of the third movie, you will have seen many things: not just battles, but changes within the characters and all kinds of surprising twists and turns.'

Cate Blanchett not only believes that the international appeal of *The Lord of the Rings Trilogy* is assured, but that the finished films will have an enduring reputation: 'So many people have said that they wanted to be part of this project because it is historic. You can sense it amongst the crew, you can feel it with the actors: this is something we know to be a once-in-a-lifetime experience. More than that, it is something that will be passed on from generation to generation.'

For Peter Jackson, as his work on these films nears completion, there still remains one more ambition: 'I'm always thinking of a day that I hope will come; a day when, at some film or video festival, people will view these three films back-to-back; when an audience will sit down and watch *The Lord of the Rings* all the way through from beginning to end. That's something to look forward to: the day when they stop being three separate movies and become one big story again!'

'One day Peter was giving some VIPs the grand tour: he showed his guests the hundreds of models, busts and statuettes lined up on shelves and he pointed out the thousands of sketches that covered the walls, from floor to ceiling. All the while he was explaining: about hobbits, Dwarves and Elves, about the Watcher in the Water, the Balrog and the Ringwraiths; he recounted the history of Middle-earth in depth and he described the different places and characters and encounters. Then he paused for a second, turned round with a big smile, and said: "You know, this would make a great book!"'

JOHN HOWE

THE LORD OF THE RINGS
THE FELLOWSHIP OF THE RING

Principal Cast

Elijah Wood, *Frodo Baggins*
Ian McKellen, *Gandalf*
Viggo Mortensen, *Aragorn*
Sean Astin, *Sam*
Liv Tyler, *Arwen*
Billy Boyd, *Pippin*
Dominic Monaghan, *Merry*
Ian Holm, *Bilbo Baggins*
Orlando Bloom, *Legolas*
Christopher Lee, *Saruman*
Cate Blanchett, *Galadriel*
Sean Bean, *Boromir*
John Rhys-Davies, *Gimli*
Hugo Weaving, *Elrond*
Andy Serkis, *Gollum/Sméagol*
Marton Csokas, *Celeborn*
Lawrence Makoare, *Lurtz*

Principal Filmmakers

Peter Jackson, Director/Writer Producer
Barrie M Osborne, Producer
Tim Sanders, Producer
Fran Walsh, Writer/Co-Producer
Philippa Boyens, Writer
Mark Ordesky, Executive Producer
Bob and Harvey Weinstein, Executive Producers
Rick Porras, Associate Producer
Ellen M Somers, Associate Producer
Andrew Lesnie, A.C.S., Director of Photography
Richard Taylor, Creature/Miniature/Armour/Special Make-up Effects Supervisor
Grant Major, Production Supervisor
Ngila Dickson, Costume Designer
Howard Shore, Composer
Jamie Selkirk, Post Production Supervisor
John Gilbert, Editor
Michael J Horton, Editor
Jim Rygiel, Visual Effects Supervisor
Alan Lee, Conceptual Artist/Set Decorator
John Howe, Conceptual Artist
Dan Hennah, Supervising Art Director
Peter Owen, Make-up and Hair Design
Peter King, Make-up and Hair Design